Understanding
Elder Abuse

Concise Guides on Trauma Care
Book Series

Understanding Elder Abuse

A Clinician's Guide

Shelly L. Jackson

American Psychological Association • Washington, DC

Published by
American Psychological Association
750 First Street, NE
Washington, DC 20002
www.apa.org

APA Order Department
P.O. Box 92984
Washington, DC 20090-2984
Tel: (800) 374-2721; Direct: (202) 336-5510
Fax: (202) 336-5502; TDD/TTY: (202) 336-6123
Online: www.apa.org/pubs/books
E-mail: order@apa.org

In the U.K., Europe, Africa, and the Middle East, copies may be ordered from
Eurospan Group
c/o Pegasus Drive
Stratton Business Park
Biggleswade Bedfordshire
SG18 8TQ United Kingdom
Tel: +44 (0) 1767 604972
Fax: +44 (0) 1767 601640
Online: https://www.eurospanbookstore.com/apa
E-mail: eurospan@turpin-distribution.com

Typeset in Minion by Circle Graphics, Inc., Columbia, MD

Printer: Sheridan Books, Chelsea, MI
Cover Designer: Mercury Publishing Services, Inc., Rockville, MD

Library of Congress Cataloging-in-Publication Data

Names: Jackson, Shelly L., author.
Title: Understanding elder abuse : a clinician's guide / Shelly L. Jackson.
Description: First edition. | Washington, DC : American Psychological
   Association, [2018] | Series: Concise guides on trauma care book series |
   Includes bibliographical references and index.
Identifiers: LCCN 2017013676 | ISBN 9781433827556 | ISBN 1433827557
Subjects: LCSH: Older people—Abuse of. | Older people—Abuse of—Prevention. |
   Abused elderly—Services for.
Classification: LCC HV6626.3 .J33 2018 | DDC 362.6/82—dc23 LC record available at
https://lccn.loc.gov/2017013676

British Library Cataloguing-in-Publication Data
A CIP record is available from the British Library.

Printed in the United States of America
First Edition

http://dx.doi.org/10.1037/0000056-000

10 9 8 7 6 5 4 3 2 1

To the adult protective services (APS) caseworkers in Virginia who shared with me their time and knowledge, and to the clients who ultimately changed my life, I am forever grateful.

Contents

Series Foreword

Exposure to traumatic events is all too common. Trauma increases the risk for a range of significant mental health problems, such as post-traumatic stress disorder (PTSD) and depression; physical health problems; negative health behaviors, such as smoking and excessive alcohol consumption; impaired social and occupational functioning; and overall lower quality of life. As mass traumas (e.g., September 11, military engagements in Iraq and Afghanistan, natural disasters such as Hurricane Katrina) have propelled trauma into a brighter public spotlight, the number of trauma survivors seeking services for mental health consequences will likely increase. Yet despite the far-ranging consequences of trauma and the high rates of exposure, relatively little emphasis is placed on trauma education in undergraduate and graduate training programs for mental health service providers in the United States. Calls for action have appeared in the American Psychological Association's journal *Psychological Trauma: Theory, Research, Practice, and Policy*, with such articles as "The Need for Inclusion of Psychological Trauma in the Professional Curriculum: A Call to Action," by Christine A. Courtois and Steven N. Gold (2009); and "The Art and Science of Trauma-Focused Training and Education" by Anne P. DePrince and Elana Newman (2011). The lack of education in the assessment and treatment of trauma-related distress and associated clinical issues at undergraduate and graduate levels increases the urgency to develop effective trauma resources for students as well as postgraduate professionals.

This book series, Concise Guides on Trauma Care, addresses that urgent need by providing truly translational books that bring the best of trauma psychology science to mental health professions working in diverse settings. To do so, the series focuses on what we know (and do not know) about specific trauma topics, with attention to how trauma psychology science translates to diverse populations (diversity broadly defined, in terms of development, ethnicity, socioeconomic status, sexual orientation, and so forth). Books in the series will address a range of assessment, treatment, and developmental issues in trauma-informed care. This series represents one of many efforts undertaken by Division 56 (Trauma Psychology) of the American Psychological Association to advance trauma training and education (e.g., see https://www.apa.org/ed/resources/trauma-competencies-training.pdf).

We are pleased to work with Division 56 and a volunteer editorial board to develop this series, which continues to advance with the publication of this important guide on elder abuse by Shelly L. Jackson. As clinicians, researchers, and policymakers increasingly turn their attention to the problem of older adult abuse and exploitation, Jackson offers a practical and accessible overview of the empirical literature. Her review of empirical work on older adult abuse integrates essential information about a host of clinically relevant topics, including reporting considerations. This practical book, grounded in research, will be of great use to mental health professionals working with older adults.

Anne P. DePrince
Ann T. Chu
Series Editors

Understanding
Elder Abuse

1

Introduction and Overview
of Elder Abuse

Given that 10,000 baby boomers turn 65 each day (Cohn & Taylor, 2010) and the power of the baby boom generation to compel social change (Van Duizend, 2008), clinicians (mental health professionals) are increasingly likely to encounter victims of elder abuse in the course of their practice or become aware of an abusive situation involving one of their clients. They will be expected to respond appropriately.

Clinicians are well-poised to meet the growing demand for expertise on preventing, identifying, and ameliorating elder abuse. Nevertheless, clinical interventions to effectively address elder abuse require greater attention and development (Moore & Browne, 2016). Specifically, interventions to help victims heal and reduce their risk of revictimization are needed, as well as interventions to alter offenders' behavior. Family therapists are needed to develop and supply therapeutic interventions when family dynamics are involved.

http://dx.doi.org/10.1037/0000056-001
Understanding Elder Abuse: A Clinician's Guide, by S. L. Jackson

As the likelihood of dementia in older adults increases with age (Plassman et al., 2007), and its prevalence is expected to grow in the coming decades (Prince et al., 2013), psychologists and neuropsychologists must generate better means of assessing the older adult's capacity in a range of domains (Blum, 2015; Demakis, 2013a; Moye & Braun, 2010), including financial capacity (Gibson & Greene, 2013; Lichtenberg, 2016; Moye & Marson, 2007), as well as provide assessments to guide guardianship proceedings (Demakis, 2012, 2016; Gibson & Greene, 2013) and determine vulnerability (Wood & Lichtenberg, 2017). Already, neuropsychologists are being recruited to serve on multidisciplinary teams that supply in-home neuropsychological evaluations of elder abuse victims (Wiglesworth, Kemp, & Mosqueda, 2008).

As more of these cases enter the criminal justice system (Navarro, Gassoumis, & Wilber, 2013), forensic psychologists can also play a critical role by conducting psychological evaluations of elder abuse offenders, providing related expert testimony (Rom-Rymer, 2006), and educating criminal justice professionals (e.g., judges) about elder abuse (Howze & White, 2010). Research and analysis by clinicians can also contribute to relevant law and policy pertaining to elder abuse (Brank, 2007; Gibson & Greene, 2013). These examples are but a few of the ways clinicians can make a positive contribution to the emerging field of elder abuse (see Gatz, Smyer, & DiGilio, 2016).

Elder abuse has occurred throughout history (Teaster, Wangmo, & Anetzberger, 2010). However, private and public attention to elder abuse is quite recent, beginning in the 1970s. Elder abuse is now a recognized phenomenon found around the world (Phelan, 2013). As of 2010, 13.0% of the U.S. population was age 65 and older, with this group expected to compose 19.3% of the population by 2030 (U.S. Census Bureau, 2012). Of those aged 60 and older, it is estimated that just over 10% experience some form of elder abuse in a given year (Acierno et al., 2010; Lachs & Berman, 2011). As the population of older adults increases (U.S. Census Bureau, 2012), so too will the numbers of those affected by elder abuse.

Although still few, there have been modest political and empirical gains since the landmark release of the Institute of Medicine's (IOM's)

Elder Mistreatment: Abuse, Neglect, and Exploitation in an Aging America (Bonnie & Wallace, 2003), which depicted the deplorable condition of the elder abuse field (e.g., Payne, 2011). The Elder Justice Act was enacted in 2009; it is the only federal legislation devoted exclusively to the problem. However, research is still in the nascent stage (Pillemer, Connolly, Breckman, Spreng, & Lachs, 2015), and Moore and Browne (2016) lamented that prevention has been all but ignored (see Nerenberg, 2008, for an exception). Furthermore, the research has been uneven, with less empirical attention to caregiver neglect (IOM, 2014) and psychological–verbal abuse (Fulmer, Rodgers, & Pelger, 2014) compared with other forms of elder abuse.

What is known about elder abuse, however, forms the substance of this book, which is designed to enable clinicians to better meet the needs of their older clients.[1] This book imparts a basic understanding of elder abuse, including risk and protective factors, the importance of cognition and capacity in this context, unique communication issues, clinicians' legal and ethical obligations, what to expect when interfacing with adult protective services (APS), available screening instruments, and current interventions. The goal is to enable clinicians to recognize and respond appropriately should they encounter an older adult who is or may be the victim of elder abuse.

The remainder of this chapter provides a broad introduction to elder abuse, including definitions, prevalence, theories, and consequences. It ends with an overview of the book.

ELDER ABUSE DEFINITIONS

Initially describing primarily physical abuse, the definition of *elder abuse* has evolved and expanded over time (Mysyuk, Westendorp, & Lindenberg, 2013). According to the Centers for Disease Control and Prevention (CDC;

---

[1] This book focuses on elder abuse occurring in domestic settings, as most clinicians will not interact with residents of long-term care facilities that primarily house the most vulnerable older adults (Castle, Ferguson-Rome, & Teresi, 2015). In addition, the federal regulation overseeing institutional settings is vast and distinguishable from policy targeting abuse in domestic settings. Assisted living and in-home care are largely unregulated (Greene, Lepore, Lux, Porter, & Freeland, 2015).

2016a), elder abuse is "an intentional act or failure to act by a caregiver or another person in a relationship involving an expectation of trust that causes or creates a risk of harm to an older adult" (p. 28). In their seminal report, Bonnie and Wallace (2003) similarly defined *elder mistreatment* as

> (a) intentional actions that cause harm or create a serious risk of harm (whether or not harm is intended) to a vulnerable elder by a caregiver or other person who stands in a trust relationship to the elder or (b) failure by a caregiver to satisfy the elder's basic needs or to protect the elder from harm. (p. 1)

One controversial aspect of these definitions is the question of whether a "trust" relationship must be present to constitute elder abuse. Conceptually, elder abuse would seem to exclude offenses perpetrated by strangers. However, Goergen and Beaulieu's (2013) eloquent analysis of this conceptualization argues that, at times, offenses perpetrated by people who are initially strangers can constitute elder abuse. For example, a dyad may meet online, and although initially strangers, part of the grooming involves becoming acquainted and eventually intimate (emotionally if not physically), as in romance scams. Although the CDC (2016a) recently released definitions, the field continues to struggle over how to define elder abuse. Garre-Olmo et al. (2009) defined elder abuse as "any action or any lack of appropriate action that causes harm, intentionally or unintentionally, to an elderly person" (p. 815), suggesting age alone is the defining characteristic of elder abuse. Age as the defining feature of elder abuse is no more controversial among professionals than it is among older adults (Mouton et al., 2005). At the most restrictive end of the spectrum, however, is Dong and Simon's (2010) definition that requires three elements: (a) older age, (b) vulnerability, and (c) the presence of a trust relationship (p. 744). This volume uses the CDC's (2016a) definition of elder abuse, necessitating the presence of a trusting relationship between the victim and offender. This definition includes not only family members but also friends, paid caregivers, financial advisors, and other professionals, depending on the situation.

Further complicating the definition is that elder abuse is a rubric under which typically five forms of elder abuse are subsumed (Dong, 2014). These five forms are financial exploitation, caregiver neglect and abandonment, psychological abuse, physical abuse, and sexual abuse. According to the CDC (2016a),[2] *financial exploitation* is defined as the illegal, unauthorized, or improper use of an older individual's resources by a caregiver or other person in a trusting relationship, for the benefit of someone other than the older individual. This includes depriving an older individual of rightful access to, information about, or use of personal benefits, resources, belongings, or assets. Signs and symptoms of financial exploitation include but are not limited to

- missing money or valuable possessions;
- appearance of previously uninvolved relatives;
- adding names on a bank account or bank signature card;
- unauthorized use of an ATM card;
- changes in a will or other financial documents; and
- unpaid bills, although there are sufficient resources.

Caregiver neglect is defined as failure by a caregiver or other person in a trust relationship to protect an elder from harm or the failure to meet needs for essential medical care, nutrition, hydration, hygiene, clothing, basic activities of daily living, or shelter, which results in a serious risk of compromised health or safety, relative to age, health status, and cultural norms. *Abandonment* has been conceptualized as an extreme form of neglect involving the desertion of a vulnerable older adult by anyone who has assumed the responsibility for care or custody of that person. Signs and symptoms of caregiver neglect include but are not limited to

- dehydration, malnutrition, untreated bed sores, and poor personal hygiene;
- unattended or untreated health problems;
- hazardous or unsafe living conditions/arrangements (e.g., improper wiring, no heat, no running water);

---

[2] In the past, abrogation of basic constitutional rights (e.g., restriction on freedom of movement; Kapp, 1995) were also considered a form of elder abuse, but that concept has disappeared in the literature.

- unsanitary and unclean living conditions (e.g., dirt, fleas, lice, soiled bedding, human or animal fecal/urine smell, inadequate clothing); and
- the desertion of an older adult at a hospital, a nursing facility, or other public place.

Physical abuse is defined as the intentional use of physical force that results in acute or chronic illness, bodily injury, physical pain, functional impairment, distress, or death. Signs and symptoms of physical abuse include but are not limited to

- bruises, black eyes, welts, cuts, and rope marks;
- broken bones, bone fractures, and skull fractures;
- open wounds, cuts, punctures, and untreated injuries in various stages of healing;
- sprains, dislocations, and internal injuries/bleeding;
- broken assistive devices (eyeglasses, dentures, walker); and
- using prescription drugs in ways other than prescribed (over- or underuse).

Psychological abuse is defined as verbal or nonverbal behavior that results in the infliction of anguish, mental pain, fear, or distress, that is perpetrated by a caregiver or other person who stands in a trust relationship to the elder.[3] Such behaviors may have immediate effects or delayed effects that are short or long term in nature that may or may not be readily apparent to or acknowledged by the victim. They may include any of the following and vary according to cultural norms: humiliation/disrespect, threats, harassment, or isolation/coercive control. Signs and symptoms of psychological abuse include, but are not limited to

- visibly emotionally upset or agitated;
- extremely withdrawn and noncommunicative or nonresponsive;
- unusual behavior usually attributed to dementia (e.g., sucking, biting, rocking); and
- the caregiver's refusal to allow visitors to see an older adult alone.

---

[3] The term *psychological abuse* is used in this volume, although studies sometimes use the terms *emotional* or *verbal abuse*.

Sexual abuse is defined as forced and/or unwanted sexual interaction (touching and nontouching acts) of any kind with an older adult. Signs and symptoms of sexual abuse include, but are not limited to

- bruises around the breasts or genital area;
- unexplained venereal disease or genital infections;
- unexplained vaginal or anal bleeding; and
- torn, stained, or bloody underclothing.

Self-Neglect

There is some debate in the field about whether *self-neglect* falls under the rubric of elder abuse (Payne & Gainey, 2005). Self-neglect is defined as an adult's inability, because of physical or mental impairment or diminished capacity, to perform essential self-care tasks, including (a) obtaining essential food, clothing, shelter, and medical care; (b) obtaining goods and services necessary to maintain physical health, mental health, or general safety; and/or (c) managing one's own financial affairs (Teaster et al., 2006). Many state statutes include self-neglect in their response to elder abuse, and it is a significant part of an APS caseworker's caseload (Teaster et al., 2006). There also is evidence that self-neglect is related to other forms of elder abuse, either as a consequence of other forms of victimization or creating a vulnerability for which an abusive individual might take advantage (Dong, Simon, & Evans, 2013; Dong et al., 2009). However, self-neglect does not involve a relationship obliged by the typical definition of elder abuse, and therefore the CDC (2016a) excludes self-neglect as a form of elder abuse. This is the position adopted in this volume.

Distinguishing Elder Abuse From Other Harms

As presented in Figure 1.1, elder abuse is distinguishable (albeit overlapping) from other harms against older adults (Heisler, 2015). Elder abuse comprises five forms: caregiver neglect and physical, financial, psychological, and sexual abuse. In contrast, *abuse in later life* forms a subset of elder abuse by its focus on domestic violence and sexual assault of older

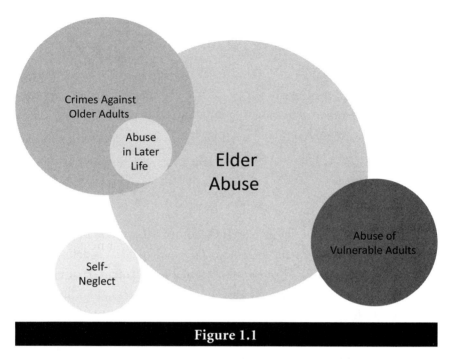

Figure 1.1

How elder abuse is distinguishable from, yet overlaps with, other harms against older adults (based on definitions in Heisler, 2015).

adults (Crockett, Brandl, & Dabby, 2015; Penhale, 2003). Thus, although overlapping to a degree with elder abuse, abuse in later life is considerably narrower and typically espouses its own theoretical position (Brandl, 2002). *Crimes against older adults*, such as burglary, assault, financial scams, and identity theft, are typically perpetrated by a stranger rather than a trusted person and therefore are typically excluded from the rubric of elder abuse (Burnes et al., 2017; Policastro, Gainey, & Payne, 2015). In addition, crimes against older adults usually garner greater attention from the discipline of criminal justice than from social work or gerontology (Payne, 2002). *Abuse of vulnerable adults* encompasses individuals ages 18 years and older with some statutorily defined vulnerability (Hughes, Lund, Gabrielli, Powers, & Curry, 2011). Thus, there is again some overlap with elder abuse given that some older victims also exhibit vulnerability, but because the category includes younger adults as well, it is distinct from elder abuse. In addition, as described earlier, elder abuse is distinguishable from self-neglect because there is no perpetrator involved.

PREVALENCE OF ELDER ABUSE

Only recently has the field been able to estimate the prevalence of elder abuse, although ongoing surveillance eludes the field (Jackson, 2017b; U.S. Government Accountability Office, 2011). As mentioned earlier, it is estimated that just over 10% of this country's adults aged 60 and older experience some form of elder abuse in a given year (Acierno et al., 2010; Lachs & Berman, 2011), although prevalence varies by the type of abuse involved: financial exploitation (5.2%), caregiver neglect (5.1%), emotional/psychological abuse (4.6%), physical abuse (1.6%), and sexual abuse (< 1.0%; Acierno et al., 2010). Although prevalence studies have been undertaken in countries around the world, these studies are not comparable because of differences in definitions, methodologies, and instruments (Cooper, Selwood, & Livingston, 2009). However, across prevalence studies, psychological abuse appears to be the most prevalent form of elder abuse (Jackson, 2016c). On the basis of APS data, between 30% and 40% of reported abused older adults experience more than one type of abuse simultaneously (Clancy, McDaid, O'Neill, & O'Brien, 2011; Teaster et al., 2006), sometimes referred to as *poly-victimization* in later life.

Very little research has included minority populations, even though approximately 20% of older adults are minorities: 8.4% African American, 6.9% Hispanic origin, 3.5% Asian or Pacific Islander, and 1% American Indian or Native Alaskan (U.S. Census Bureau, 2012). However, there is some evidence that rates of some types of abuse are higher among minority populations. Several studies have found that African American individuals are more likely to be financially exploited than Caucasian American individuals (Beach, Schulz, Castle, & Rosen, 2010; Laumann, Leitsch, & Waite, 2008; Peterson et al., 2014). For example, in a county-level self-report prevalence study, Beach et al. (2010) found that in the past 6 months, 12.9% of African American individuals were financially exploited compared with

2.4% of non–African American individuals. In addition, it has been suggested that among Native Alaskan persons, financial exploitation is the most frequently reported form of elder abuse (Graves, Rosich, McBride, Charles, & LaBelle, 2010). In a convenience sample of Latino immigrants residing in Los Angeles, California, using *promotores* (specially trained lay community members who provide health care education to community members), 40.4% had experienced some type of elder abuse in the previous year (DeLiema, Gassoumis, Homeier, & Wilber, 2012), a rate significantly higher than nationally representative prevalence studies find, although this higher rate is accounted for in part by the voluntary nature of the sample.

LOCATION OF ELDER ABUSE

Although elder abuse occurs in long-term care facilities (Castle, Ferguson-Rome, & Teresi, 2015), and these instances certainly receive more political attention (Jackson, 2017b), the majority of reported elder abuse (89.3%) occurs among older adults residing in the community (Clancy et al., 2011; Teaster et al., 2006), most typically in their place of residence. Contrary to stereotypes of aging, the majority (95%) of older adults reside in the community (U.S. Census Bureau, 2012). In fact, only 3.6% (1.5 million) of older adults aged 65 and older reside in a nursing home (Administration on Aging, 2012). However, the proportion clearly increases with age: 15.1% are under age 65, 16.1% are ages 65 to 74, 27.2% are ages 75 to 84, and 41.6% are ages 85 or older (CDC, 2016b, p. 105).

UNDERREPORTING OF ELDER ABUSE

There is a broad consensus that elder abuse is underreported. A comparison of self-reported abuse to official reports in New York state concluded that one in 24 cases of elder abuse is reported to authorities (Lachs & Berman, 2011). However, there were differences depending on the type of abuse involved: one in 57 cases of neglect, one in 44 cases of financial exploitation, one in 20 cases of physical abuse/sexual abuse, and one in 12 cases of psychological abuse were reported to a state authority.

REVIEW OF EXISTING THEORIES

Elder abuse research is characterized by an absence of theory (National Institute of Justice [NIJ], 2014). Furthermore, when theory is invoked, the theories are frequently borrowed or adapted from the fields of child abuse or intimate partner violence. Kapp (1995), however, censured the field for borrowing concepts, asserting that elder mistreatment is a "unique problem" (p. 379). More recently, scholars have admonished the field for failing to develop elder abuse theories, generally (Bonnie & Wallace, 2003), and for distinct types of abuse, specifically (Jackson & Hafemeister, 2013d). Different theories implicate different interventions (Eisikovits, Koren, & Band-Winterstein, 2013; Jackson & Hafemeister, 2013d; Payne, 2011). For example, if it is believed that the underlying cause of elder abuse is patriarchy, the intervention might include correcting misperceptions through intensive psychoeducation for abusers as observed in the intimate partner violence field (Gondolf, 2011). Alternatively, if abusers have unresolved psychological problems, then the intervention might include addressing those unresolved problems through psychotherapy (Dutton, 2006). If, on the other hand, abusers are deviant, then the criminal justice system may be the intervention of choice, as articulated by Pillemer (2005).

In their review, Burnight and Mosqueda (2011) concluded that elder abuse theories are predominately interpersonal in nature, although other applications involve sociocultural, macrolevel, and multisystemic approaches. On the basis of a review of the literature (Burnight & Mosqueda, 2011; IOM, 2014; NIJ, 2014; Payne, 2011; Wilber & McNeilly, 2001), a brief summary of the predominant theories is presented on the following pages. Note that many theories focus on physical abuse and hold little relevance for caregiver neglect, financial exploitation, or sexual abuse, perhaps because these adapted theories initially were developed to explain other phenomena.

Interpersonal Theories

Caregiver Stress Theory

Caregiver stress theory is perhaps the only theory originating within the field itself. Elder abuse occurs when family members caring for an impaired older adult are unable to adequately manage their caregiving responsibilities (Steinmetz, 1978). The older victim is typically described as highly dependent on the caregiver, who becomes overwhelmed, frustrated, and abusive because of the unrelenting caretaking demands posed by the dependent older person. Prominent in the 1970s, this unidimensional theory has fallen out of favor among scholars (Bonnie & Wallace, 2003), although practitioners continue to find this concept relevant (Sanders, 2016). To address caregiver stress, practitioners have focused interventions primarily on alleviating caregiver stress through respite care or teaching caregivers coping strategies (Doty, 2010). Caregiver stress interventions are unequivocally the most prevalent form of elder abuse intervention (Ayalon, Lev, Green, & Nevo, 2016).

Family Power-Dependent Relationship Model

Integrating concepts from gerontology and intimate partner violence, Ziminski Pickering and Phillips (2014) recently introduced a model for the development of aggression (physical and verbal) toward older parents by their adult children. The model posits that long before a caregiving situation arises, there exists a cognitively intact older adult and a dependent adult child. Families are by their nature interdependent, but at some point the adult child perceives a power deficit and uses aggression in an attempt to claim more power in the relationship. No elder abuse interventions have been developed based on this theory.

Intergenerational Transmission of Violence Model

The intergenerational transmission of violence theory, based on social learning theory, posits that abusive acts are a learned behavior transferred through the process of modeling (Bandura, 1973). Elder abuse occurs as a result of the abusive individual's having learned to use violence in an earlier familial context, either to resolve conflicts or to gain a desired outcome

(Wilber & McNeilly, 2001). Korbin, Anetzberger, and Austin (1995), however, found little empirical support for the intergenerational transmission model in the context of elder abuse. No elder abuse interventions have been developed on the basis of this model.

Social Exchange Theory

For the social exchange theory, practitioners argue that social behavior involves negotiated exchanges of material and nonmaterial goods. Abusive individuals perceive themselves as not receiving their fair share from a relationship with the older person and therefore resort to violence in an effort to restore or obtain equilibrium within the relationship (Decalmer & Glendenning, 1993). This theory may hold less relevance for elder abuse, particularly where parent–adult child relationships are at play in which choice is not the defining characteristic of the relationship (Rusbult & Van Lange, 2003). No elder abuse interventions have been developed on the basis of this theory.

Dyadic Discord Theory

The dyadic discord theory combines elements from two theories. Relationship discord results from a combination of contextual factors such as a history of family violence, which primes a person's acceptance of violence as a conflict resolution strategy (i.e., social learning theory), and situational factors such as a lack of relationship satisfaction (i.e., social exchange theory; Riggs & O'Leary, 1989). However, this theory may hold less relevance for an abusive situation involving an older parent and an adult child where the relationships tend to be more needs-based than contribution- or choice-based (Maccoby, 2000). No elder abuse interventions have been developed on the basis of this theory.

Sociocultural Theories

Power and Control Theory

The power and control theory posits that abusive individuals use coercive tactics to gain and maintain power and control during the course of a relationship with another individual (Yllo & Bogard, 1998). This feminist theory asserts that because males have more power in our society, they are more likely to use coercive tactics to maintain control (Brandl, 2002). Dominant in the domestic violence field, the power and control theory has been critiqued for being unidimensional and its inability to explain the various subtypes of elder abuse. On the basis of this theory, psycho-educational interventions such as batterer intervention programs are prolific in the context of domestic violence (Gondolf, 2011), with only one such intervention targeting individuals who are physically abusive toward older women (Klein, Tobin, Salomon, & Dubois, 2008).

Routine Activities Theory

A frequently invoked theory to explain elder abuse is the criminological routine activities theory (RAT). Designed to explain opportunistic crime, the theory posits that crime results when there is (a) a suitable target, (b) an unguarded target, and (c) a motivated offender. Used primarily in the context of financial exploitation (e.g., Setterlund, Tilse, Wilson, McCawley, & Rosenman, 2007), a suitable target might be an older person who appears vulnerable in some way (i.e., suitable), particularly in the absence of a friend or family member (i.e., unguarded), who is in the presence of a motivated offender. When these three elements converge, elder abuse may occur. RAT has been critiqued, however, as rather superficial; for example, RAT does not address the motivation of the offender. However, it does offer simple solutions to crime prevention, such as providing oversight for older adults. Indeed, there is a call for adult children to play a greater oversight role in their parents' financial matters (Huddleston, 2011).

Macrolevel Theory

Ageism

Ageism involves negative attitudes toward older adults and contributes to apathy toward their maltreatment (Harbison, 2016; Phelan, 2008). Facets of ageism include talking with an older adult in a loud or baby voice or acting as a protector rather than an equal (Hagestad & Uhlenberg, 2005). Through the lens of ageism, it is argued that younger adults have power based on their youth, whereas older individuals have less power based on their older age; therefore, younger adults perceive older adults as different and inferior. These negative stereotypes (e.g., useless, functionally impaired) limit both how younger adults view older adults and how some older adults perceive themselves. Individuals are more likely to invoke stereotypes with strangers than with people they know, such as their grandparents (Hagestad & Uhlenberg, 2005). Therefore, one antidote to ageism is simply exposure to older people. Indeed, perceiving ageism as detrimental to society, the World Health Organization (WHO) recently initiated the #YearsAhead campaign targeting the elimination of ageism by dispelling stereotypes through Instagram (WHO, 2015).

Multisystemic Models

Biopsychosocial Model

The biopsychosocial model asserts that elder abuse is attributable to multiple factors simultaneously. The causal mechanisms include the characteristics of both the older person and the abusive individual, each of whom is embedded in a larger sociocultural context (family and friends) and their status inequality, relationship type, and power and exchange dynamics (Bonnie & Wallace, 2003, p. 63). Although such a model provides ample points for intervention, it has not been empirically tested, and no elder abuse intervention based on this model has been developed.

Ecological Model

The ecological model posits that influences at the individual, relationship, community, and societal levels contribute to the occurrence of elder abuse (Schiamberg & Gans, 2000; Von Heydrich, Schiamberg, & Chee, 2012). For example, factors at the individual level might include the degree of dependency of the older adult and the degree of the adult child's impairment (e.g., substance abuse). At the relationship level, factors might include the quality of the relationship between the older adult and adult child. At the community level, factors might include the degree of neighborhood cohesion in which the older adult lives. Finally, at the societal level, factors might include ageism or whether social policies are in place that facilitate older adults remaining in their own home and thus reducing their reliance on unsuitable family members for assistance. Interventions adopting this model might target pliable risk factors at the various levels. However, no such elder abuse intervention exists.

Is There a Predominant Theory?

It would be inaccurate to say that any one of these theories garners more support than another. As noted, the field is predominately atheoretical. Theories have typically attempted to explain "elder abuse" rather than forms of elder abuse. Furthermore, the role ethnicity plays in theory has been limited. Parra-Cardona, Meyer, Schiamberg, and Post (2007), however, adapted the ecological model to arrange risk factors among Latino families experiencing elder abuse. For example, factors at the individual level included the degree of dependency of the older adult but also their country of origin as well as the degree of the adult child's impairment (e.g., substance abuse). At the relationship level, factors included the quality of the relationship between the older adult and adult child as well as family distrust toward institutions. At the community level, factors included the degree of economic opportunity and limited access to institutional support in the community in which they live. Finally, at the societal level, factors included an anti-immigrant climate and economic instability. Clearly, there remain significant gaps in our understanding of elder abuse among minority populations (Moore & Browne, 2016).

CONSEQUENCES

Only recently have studies identified different types of harms that mistreated older persons may suffer. There is some evidence that consequences vary by subtype (Burnett et al., 2016; Dong & Simon, 2013a, 2013b). For example, Burnett et al. (2016) found higher rates of mortality for victims of caregiver neglect and financial exploitation compared with physical abuse and psychological abuse. Nonetheless, the consequences of elder abuse routinely lead to a diminished quality of life for all abused older adults. Unfortunately, whether and how consequences of elder abuse differ across minority populations is currently unknown.

The consequences associated with elder abuse can be devastating and are typically categorized as psychological, social, health, financial, secondary victims, and costs to society (Bonnie & Wallace, 2003). Below is a brief review of research on these consequences, along with a discussion of consequences for undergoing an investigation by APS.

Psychological

Elder abuse can be characterized as a stressful life event or as a traumatic event resulting in psychological distress (Roepke-Buehler, Simon, & Dong, 2015). Although a sophisticated understanding of the psychological effects associated with elder abuse eludes us (although see Ogle, Rubin, & Siegler, 2013), across several studies, using different samples and measures, depression has been consistently associated with elder abuse. Roepke-Buehler et al. (2015) measured depression with the Center for Epidemiologic Studies Depression Scale (CES-D; Kohout, Berkman, Evans, & Cornoni-Huntley, 1993), while Dong, Simon, Odwazny, and Gorbien (2008) and Garre-Olmo et al. (2009) used the five-item Geriatric Depression Scale to measure depression. Dong et al. (2008) found that after adjusting for age and sex, participants with depression were more likely to report abuse and neglect. Cisler, Begle, Amstadter, and Acierno (2012) measured emotional symptoms with two unstandardized questions (i.e., a combination of emotional symptoms including anxiety, depression, or irritability, and functional impairment due to personal or emotional problems). Compared with physical and sexual abuse, emotional abuse (and history of prior trauma events exposure, poor physical health, younger age, low social support, and needing help with activities of daily living) was related to emotional symptoms (defined above), suggesting that emotional abuse has a more direct effect on mental health.

Social

Social consequences have also been identified, but much less is known about them. Disruptions in social and family relationships occur as a consequence of elder abuse (Jackson & Hafemeister, 2010), which can be psychologically devastating. For example, if family members are concerned about a loved one, but the older adult refuses to change their situation, family members may become angry or discouraged and cut off ties with the older adult (Breckman & Adelman, 1988).

Health

The health consequences of elder abuse are many. They may include compromised health (Gibbs, 2014), resulting directly or indirectly from elder abuse. For example, physical injury can result directly from physical abuse, sexual abuse, and caregiver neglect (Murphy, Waa, Jaffer, Sauter, & Chan, 2013). Several forms of elder abuse have been associated with hospitalization (Dong & Simon, 2013b) and even mortality (Dong et al., 2009; Burnett et al., 2016). Indirect effects of elder abuse on health might include, for example, when financial exploitation results in the inability to purchase medications or pay for health care services (Price, King, Dillard, & Bulot, 2011). Financial strain associated with financial exploitation may produce stress (Sapolsky, Armanini, Packan, & Tombaugh, 1987), which is associated with decreased mental and physical health (Kahn & Pearlin, 2006) and higher mortality (Szanton et al., 2008). Furthermore, recovery from the neglect or physical abuse tends to be more difficult for older adults who typically have fewer physical reserves (Horan & Clague, 1999).

Financial

The financial consequences are many as well. Victims of financial exploitation, for example, may experience major or minor financial loss (Holtfreter, Reisig, Mears, & Wolfe, 2014). Financial loss may occur in the form of cold cash but may extend to loss of assets including one's home (Jackson & Hafemeister, 2012b), with some older adults having to move into senior subsidized housing (Jackson & Hafemeister, 2010). One issue many victims of financial exploitation face is tarnished credit scores and consequent difficulty obtaining credit or unrelenting calls from debt collectors (Deem, 2000). Furthermore, financial burden can be incurred through medical bills and the need to purchase new assistive devices as a result of other forms of maltreatment (Payne, 2011).

Secondary Victims

There are secondary victims as well. Family members are often aware of an ongoing abusive situation and must bear witness to it (Breckman & Adelman, 1988; Jackson & Hafemeister, 2015). In addition, family members may become financially responsible for older adults who have lost some or all of their life savings or who become dependent because of maltreatment that compromises their health or physical functioning (Bond, Cuddy, Dixon, Duncan, & Smith, 2000). Finally, for those who have lost their entire life savings, family members will have lost their inheritance.

Costs to Society

Elder abuse imposes significant costs to society as well. For example, there are many agencies that might respond to elder abuse (e.g., emergency medical technicians, civil legal assistance, aging services network), increasing the financial burden to society. Furthermore, as a result of financial exploitation, some older adults may become eligible for Medicaid, also increasing the costs to society (U.S. Senate Special Committee on Aging, 2011).

Consequences Associated With an APS Investigation

Perhaps more as a result of interfacing with the social services system than the experience of elder abuse per se (i.e., outcomes of an APS investigation), older victims may experience reductions or restrictions on their independence designed to increase their safety (Choi, Kulick, & Mayer, 1999). At the most extreme, this reduction might take the form of imposition of a guardian (Jackson & Hafemeister, 2013b), perhaps the most draconian outcome for older adults as their decision-making freedom is stripped away (Wright, 2010). Changes in living arrangements also may occur—either institutionalization (Dong & Simon, 2013a) or some less extreme change, such as a new apartment (Clancy et al., 2011; Jackson & Hafemeister, 2013b). Either way, changes in living arrangements constitute a challenging adjustment for many older adults (Hooyman & Kiyak, 1988), especially those who have lived in the same home for decades with its familiarity and memories.

CONCLUSION

Considerable gains have been made in the field of elder abuse (research, practice, and policy) since the 1970s, with progress unequivocally accelerating since 2003. For example, the Elder Justice Act was passed in 2009; it was the first federal legislation devoted exclusively to elder abuse. However, elder abuse is not widely recognized as a social problem in our country, with the possible exception of financial exploitation (Jackson, 2016b). Although our knowledge base is growing, it remains uneven and incomplete. The field has yet to rally around a set of definitions, develop thoughtful and useful theories, or more carefully identify the consequences associated with elder abuse. Each of these gaps needs filling to more thoughtfully and effectively intervene in the lives of older Americans.

In the meantime, clinicians have older clients in need of assistance. In the chapters to come, clinicians will learn the practical lessons they did not learn in graduate school. This learning includes the risk and protective factors for elder abuse (Chapter 2); the important role of cognitive capacity and how to communicate with older adults who have cognitive or other impairments (Chapter 3); how to detect elder abuse and meet one's legal and ethical obligations upon detection (Chapter 4); how to work with APS (Chapter 5); and an overview of the most current elder abuse interventions that might be useful in clinical practice (Chapter 6). The immediate goal of this book is to enable clinicians to enhance their practice with victims of elder abuse, but ultimately, the goal is to enrich the lives of older adults by ensuring that the professionals who work with them are well prepared to do so.

2

Risk and Protective Factors

Clinicians should be familiar with the body of risk and protective factors that may alert clinicians to the possibility of elder abuse. For example, across types of elder abuse, the majority of victims know their offenders (Krienert, Walsh, & Turner, 2009; Lachs & Berman, 2011; Schafer & Koltai, 2014; Teaster et al., 2006), and many victims choose to remain in ongoing and long-term relationships with them (Harbison, Coughlan, Karabanow, & VanderPlaat, 2005). Thus, characteristics and conditions of both the victim and the perpetrator can contribute to an incident of elder abuse. Undoubtedly, the greatest focus of elder abuse research has been on the identification of risk factors (i.e., factors that increase the odds of some phenomenon such as elder abuse). This chapter provides a brief review of this literature. Organized around an ecological framework (Johannesen & LoGiudice, 2013; Penhale, 2010; Schiamberg & Gans, 2000), the chapter begins with a review of individual- and relationship-level risk factors

http://dx.doi.org/10.1037/0000056-002
Understanding Elder Abuse: A Clinician's Guide, by S. L. Jackson

associated with specific types of abuse and concludes with brief remarks regarding community- and societal-level variables which, unfortunately, are scant and not differentiated by type of abuse.

INDIVIDUAL- AND RELATIONSHIP-LEVEL RISK AND PROTECTIVE FACTORS BY TYPE OF ABUSE

Much of the elder abuse research has focused on the identification of individual-level risk factors, both in the United States and around the world (e.g., Garre-Olmo et al., 2009; Gil et al., 2015; Lindert et al., 2013; Macassa et al., 2013; Yan, Chan, & Tiwari, 2015). Risk indicators are often confused with correlates of abuse. For example, although in absolute numbers women are often found to be abused more frequently than men, gender itself is not a risk factor for abuse (Reis & Nahmiash, 1998; see also Kosberg, 2014). Historically, the field has tended to lump all forms of elder abuse together when identifying risk factors. For example, Johannesen and LoGiudice (2013) completed the most comprehensive review of the elder abuse risk factor literature, identifying over 50 risk factors for elder abuse, although only 13 were found consistently across studies.

However, risk factors associated with "elder abuse" as a general category (as opposed to a specific type of elder abuse) are misleading. Research confirms that risk factors are differentially associated with types of abuse (Acierno et al., 2010; Gil et al., 2015; Jackson & Hafemeister, 2011; O'Keeffe et al., 2007; Wu et al., 2012). For example, Dong, Simon, and Evans (2012) reported that physical decline was related to psychological abuse and caregiver neglect but not to financial exploitation. Acierno et al. (2010) found that although low social support was related to caregiver neglect and physical, sexual, and emotional abuse, it was not related to financial exploitation (by a family member). In addition, O'Keeffe et al. (2007) found that living alone was related to financial exploitation but not to physical and psychological abuse (which they referred to as *interpersonal abuse*), while cohabitation was related to physical abuse. It is worth mentioning that how cohabitation comes about has implications for the potentially abusive situation. When adult offspring move in with their parents, they typically are not doing so to provide care for their older parents, but to receive needed assistance (Smits, Van Gaalen, & Mulder, 2010), a situation characteristic of physical abuse. However, when older parents move in with adult offspring, it is generally because the parents are highly vulnerable and dependent as the result of health problems or poverty and lack spouses or someone to care for them in their home (Smits et al., 2010), a living arrangement characteristic of caregiver neglect. Both situations involve cohabitation, but clinicians will want to learn how the cohabitation came about.

The body of risk factor research by type of abuse is summarized in Table 2.1 and includes only studies that differentiated among types of abuse or identified a specific type of abuse.[1] A cursory view of Table 2.1 confirms the assertion that risk factors differ across four types of abuse (no studies identifying risk factors associated with the sexual abuse of older adults exists). Some general observations are noteworthy.

Physical Abuse

Physical abuse can range in severity from a spit in the face to life-threatening assaults, and in the context of elder abuse, it may include using physical restraints (Centers for Disease Control and Prevention, 2016a). According to a review of the literature, the predominant perpetrators of physical abuse are spouses, followed by adult children (Jackson, 2016a), consistent with the finding that these perpetrators are on average slightly older than offenders in other categories because of the inclusion of spouses or partners (Jackson & Hafemeister, 2011; O'Keeffe et al., 2007). Approximately half are men, and some tend to be characterized by substance abuse, mental illness and personality disorders, relationship disturbances, and a criminal history resulting in their dependency and consequently their receipt of physical and financial care from the older victim.

Taken together, victim risk factors for physical abuse are somewhat inconsistent at this point. Although physical abuse by a spouse describes some of these cases, the emerging picture suggests that a sizable minority

---

[1]Not all studies compared all five types of abuse (e.g., Von Heydrich, Schiamberg, & Chee, 2012, included only physical abuse), and not all studies included the same set of variables.

Table 2.1

Risk and Protective Factors by Type of Abuse

Risk or protective factor	Financial exploitation	Caregiver neglect	Psychological abuse	Physical abuse
		Type of abuse		
		Victim demographic risk factors		
Age (older)	Choi & Mayer, 2000; Garre-Olmo et al., 2009; Jackson & Hafemeister, 2011	O'Keeffe et al., 2007		Lindert et al., 2012
Gender (female)	ns (Acierno et al., 2010; Holtfreter et al., 2014; Laumann et al., 2008)	males (Beach et al., 2005; Wu et al., 2012); females (Lindert et al., 2013; O'Keeffe et al., 2007); ns (Acierno et al., 2010)		Lindert et al., 2012; ns (Acierno et al., 2010)
Education	ns (Laumann et al., 2008)			
Not married (widowed, separated, divorced)	Garre-Olmo et al., 2009; Lindert et al., 2013; O'Keeffe et al., 2007; Peterson et al., 2014		Wu et al., 2012	
Low income	Peterson et al., 2014	Acierno et al., 2010; Oh et al., 2006		Mouton et al., 2004; ns (Acierno et al., 2010)
Race (African American or minority status)	Beach et al., 2010; Lauman et al., 2008; Peterson et al., 2014	Acierno et al., 2010; Amstadter, Cisler, et al., 2011	Beach et al., 2010	ns (Acierno et al., 2010; Mouton et al., 2004)

Service occupation		ns (Mouton et al., 2004)		Mouton et al., 2004
Living alone	Jackson & Hafemeister, 2011; O'Keeffe et al., 2007			Lindert et al., 2013; Mouton et al., 2004; Wu et al., 2012
Living with other family members	Beach et al., 2010; Oh et al., 2006		Garre-Olmo et al., 2009	
Living in a rented unit				Macassa et al., 2013
Home ownership	Choi et al., 1999; Choi & Mayer, 2000			
Unemployed				Acierno et al., 2010
Victim clinical risk factors				
Previous traumatic event	ns (Acierno et al., 2010)	ns (Acierno et al., 2010)	ns (Acierno et al., 2010)	ns (Acierno et al., 2010)
Depression	Beach et al., 2010	Fulmer et al., 2005; O'Keeffe et al., 2007; Wu et al., 2012	Beach et al., 2010; Garre-Olmo et al., 2009; Wu et al., 2012	Jackson & Hafemeister, 2011; Friedman et al., 2011; Wu et al., 2012
Anxiety and somatic complaints			Macassa et al., 2013	
Substance use or abuse				
Drinking alcohol			Macassa et al., 2013	Friedman et al., 2011
Low social support (or lack of a trusted other)	Acierno et al., 2010; Amstadter, Cisler, et al., 2011; Garre-Olmo et al., 2009	Acierno et al., 2010; Amstadter, Cisler, et al., 2011; Garre-Olmo et al., 2009	Acierno et al., 2010; Amstadter, Cisler, et al., 2011; Garre-Olmo et al., 2009; Melchiorre et al., 2013	Acierno et al., 2010

(continues)

Table 2.1
Risk and Protective Factors by Type of Abuse (*Continued*)

Risk or protective factor	Financial exploitation	Caregiver neglect	Psychological abuse	Physical abuse
			Type of abuse	
Larger social network	Beach, Schulz, & Sneed, 2016; Holtfreter et al., 2014			
History of child maltreatment		Fulmer et al., 2005		Jackson & Hafemeister, 2011
Self-neglect	Dong, Simon, & Evans, 2013	Dong, Simon, & Evans, 2013		ns (Dong, Simon, & Evans, 2013)
Accessed services in the past		O'Keeffe et al., 2007		
Inability to manage finances	Choi et al., 1999			
Victim health risk factors				
Diminished cognition	Choi & Mayer, 2000; Choi et al., 1999; Dong et al., 2011, Garre-Olmo et al., 2009; O'Keeffe et al., 2007; ns (Beach et al., 2010; Jackson & Hafemeister, 2011; Laumann et al., 2008)	Dong et al., 2011; Fulmer et al., 2005	Dong et al., 2011; Wang, 2006	Dong et al., 2011

(continues)

Poor health	O'Keeffe et al., 2007; ns (Acierno et al., 2010)	Acierno et al., 2010; Amstadter et al., 2010; Jackson & Hafemeister, 2011; O'Keeffe et al., 2007		ns (Acierno et al., 2010)
Chronic disease			Acierno et al., 2010; Amstadter et al., 2011; Dong et al., 2012; Garre-Olmo et al., 2009; Wu et al., 2012; Wang, 2006	
Dependency		Jackson & Hafemeister, 2011		ns (Jackson & Hafemeister, 2011)
Needs help with ADLs or IADLs		Beach et al., 2005; Garre-Olmo et al., 2009; Jackson & Hafemeister, 2011; Oh et al., 2006		
Need for ADL Assistance	Acierno et al., 2010; Amstadter et al., 2010; Amstadter et al., 2011; Wu et al., 2012; ns (Choi et al., 1999; Jackson & Hafemeister, 2011)		Acierno et al., 2010; Amstadter et al., 2010; Dong et al., 2012; Garre-Olmo et al., 2009; Wu et al., 2012; Wang, 2006	
Needs IADL assistance	Beach et al., 2010; Peterson et al., 2014			
Poor physical performance	ns (Dong et al., 2012)[a]	Dong et al., 2012	Acierno et al., 2010; Amstadter et al., 2010; Dong et al., 2012; Garre-Olmo et al., 2009; Wu et al., 2012; Wang, 2006	

29

Table 2.1
Risk and Protective Factors by Type of Abuse (*Continued*)

Risk or protective factor	Type of abuse			
	Financial exploitation	Caregiver neglect	Psychological abuse	Physical abuse
Physical disability			Acierno et al., 2010; Amstadter et al., 2010; Dong et al., 2012; Garre-Olmo et al., 2009; Wang, 2006; Wu et al., 2012	
Frequent use of health care services			Macassa et al., 2013	
Victim protective factors				
Living alone		ns (Mouton et al., 2004)		Mouton et al., 2004
Perceived health	Laumann et al., 2008			
Absence of child maltreatment	Jackson & Hafemeister, 2011			
Married	Laumann et al., 2008; Peterson et al., 2014			
Never married or widowed			Beach et al., 2010; Lindert et al., 2013; Mouton et al., 2004	
Older age			Beach et al., 2010; Macassa et al., 2013; Mouton et al., 2004	

Black and Asian Pacific Islanders			Mouton et al., 2004
Absence of financial strain			Macassa et al., 2013
Drink < 1 alcoholic drink per week			Mouton et al., 2004
High social support			Macassa et al., 2013
Perpetrator demographic risk factors			
Less than a high school education	Beach et al., 2005		
Married	Beach et al., 2010		
Related to victim			Amstadter et al., 2010
Cohabiting with the victim		ns (Jackson & Hafemeister, 2011; O'Keeffe et al., 2007)	Amstadter et al., 2010; Clancy et al., 2011; O'Keeffe et al., 2007
Perpetrator clinical risk factors			
History of child maltreatment (Neglect)	Fulmer et al., 2005		
Receives care from victim		ns (Jackson & Hafemeister, 2011; O'Keeffe et al., 2007)	O'Keeffe et al., 2007

(continues)

Table 2.1

Risk and Protective Factors by Type of Abuse (*Continued*)

	Type of abuse			
Risk or protective factor	Financial exploitation	Caregiver neglect	Psychological abuse	Physical abuse
Substance abuse	O'Keeffe et al., 2007	ns (Hwalek et al., 1996)	Hwalek et al., 1996	Amstadter et al., 2010; Homer & Gilleard, 1990; Hwalek et al., 1996; Von Heydrich et al., 2012
Depressive symptoms		Beach et al., 2005	Homer & Gilleard, 1990	
Anxiety			Homer & Gilleard, 1990	
Serious mental illness				Band-Winterstein et al., 2016; Labrum & Solomon, 2015
Personality disorders				Amstadter et al., 2010; Homer & Gilleard, 1990; Labrum & Solomon, 2015
Mutually abusive				Homer & Gilleard, 1990

Parasitic			Jackson & Hafemeister, 2011
Relationship disturbances/IPV	O'Keeffe et al., 2007		Jackson & Hafemeister, 2011; O'Keeffe et al., 2007
Criminal justice involvement			Amstadter et al., 2010
Chronic unemployment	ns (O'Keeffe et al., 2007)		
Socially dysfunctional		Homer & Gilleard, 1990	
Overburdened caretaker		Jackson & Hafemeister, 2011	
Financial problems			
Gambling	O'Keeffe et al., 2007		
		Perpetrator health risk factors	
Impaired cognitive status		Beach et al., 2005	ns (Beach et al., 2005)
Physical symptoms		Beach et al., 2005	
Unmet needs		Fulmer et al., 2005	
Unmet IADLs		Fulmer et al., 2005	

(continues)

Table 2.1
Risk and Protective Factors by Type of Abuse (*Continued*)

Risk or protective factor	Type of abuse			
	Financial exploitation	Caregiver neglect	Psychological abuse	Physical abuse
Relationship risk factors				
Poor family relationship	Oh et al., 2006	Oh et al., 2006	Oh et al., 2006	Oh et al., 2006
Poor quality victim–offender relationship		Jackson & Hafemeister, 2016; Homer & Gilleard, 1990	Homer & Gilleard, 1990	Jackson & Hafemeister, 2011; Von Heydrich et al., 2012
Victim–offender social isolation				Von Heydrich et al., 2012
External financial problems				Von Heydrich et al., 2012

Note. ADL = activities of daily living; IADL = instrumental activities of daily living; IPV = intimate partner violence; ns = not significant.
[a]Poor physical performance (tandem stand, timed walk, and ability to rise to a standing position from a chair), poorer Katz ADL score (limitations in an individual's ability to perform six basic self-care tasks: bathing, dressing, toileting, transferring, continence, and feeding), poorer Nagi score (five activities of upper or lower extremity function), and poorer Rosow and Breslau score (ability to do heavy work around the house, walk up and down stairs, and walk half a mile; Dong, Simon, & Evans, 2012).

(e.g., 39%) are providing care for a dysfunctional adult child as alluded to earlier (O'Keeffe et al., 2007). Contrary to the stereotype of the frail older adult, at least some older victims of physical abuse are relatively robust. Although more women are the victims of physical abuse, gender does not emerge as a significant risk factor across studies using multivariate analyses. It is not surprising that physical abuse is associated with a poor-quality victim–perpetrator relationship (Jackson & Hafemeister, 2011; Von Heydrich et al., 2012). The only protective factor among women is living alone, in which case an older woman is half as likely to be physically abused (Mouton et al., 2004).

Older adults may be both victims and initiators of physical violence. Perpetrators with a personality disorder have been shown to respond violently to limit setting by the older adult (Jackson & Hafemeister, 2016; Labrum, 2017). By their own admission, older victims are at times initiators of physical abuse against their offenders (Jackson & Hafemeister, 2011). This form of aggression should be differentiated from the case of patient-generated physical violence directed toward a caretaker, a well-known symptom of Alzheimer's disease (Dong, Chen, & Simon, 2014; Wiglesworth et al., 2010). Patient-generated aggression is thought to provoke violence by a caregiver. Although there is general agreement that caregiving for individuals with dementia is challenging (Pinquart & Sörensen, 2003), across several studies caregiver stress is not related to physical abuse, although it is related to other subtypes of elder abuse (Gainey & Payne, 2006; Yan, 2014; Yan & Kwok, 2011).

Caregiver Neglect

Unique to caregiver neglect is that the older adult must have had some physical or cognitive vulnerability and someone must have explicitly or implicitly assumed responsibility for their care. Being a relative of the older adult does not automatically convey a legal obligation to provide care (even for a parent). It is only once someone has assumed that responsibility that proper and ongoing care is then required (Brank & Wylie, 2016).

Society has settled on a set of activities that a person must be able to master to live independently in the community. According to gerontologists, one set of activities is referred to as *activities of daily living* (ADLs) and includes self-feeding, bathing, dressing, grooming, and toileting. Another set of higher order activities is referred to as *instrumental activities of daily living* (IADLs) and includes shopping, use of the telephone, travel in the community, financial management, housekeeping, preparing meals, and taking medications correctly (Millán-Calenti et al., 2010). Generally, older adults are able to maintain ADLs longer than IADLs. Actions that might constitute neglect include deprivation of assistance needed for ADLs or IADLs. Cases of caregiver neglect can range in severity from minor inadequate nutrition to horrific and painful pressure ulcers (bedsores) to the bone resulting from lack of care.

Perpetrators of caregiver neglect are most frequently adult children, spouses, and professional (paid) caretakers (Jackson, 2016a). They are both male and female, and about half (45%) live with the victim (Clancy, McDaid, O'Neill, & O'Brien, 2011). That perpetrators have unmet needs for assistance with ADLs and IADLs (Fulmer et al., 2005) suggests that some perpetrators are spouses with their own health issues.

Victim variables associated with caregiver neglect are many and varied, but in sum, they indicate that these victims tend to have significant physical, health, and cognitive issues resulting in their dependency (a requirement for the definition of caregiver neglect). The results for gender are mixed, but generally, gender is not a significant predictor of caregiver neglect. However, protective factors may include oldest–old age and being Hispanic (Burnes et al., 2015).

Financial Exploitation

Although considerable attention has been paid to financial scams (including consumer fraud) against older adults (Burnes et al., 2017; Holtfreter, Reisig, Mears, & Wolfe, 2014), this chapter excludes financial crimes against older adults perpetrated by strangers, while recognizing the seriousness of financial fraud (Button, Lewis, & Tapley, 2014). Financial exploitation is a term under which both illegal and improper actions are subsumed (Jackson, 2015b). It can range from theft of $20, to an entire estate worth millions, to a daughter living off of her elderly parents.

The perpetrators of financial exploitation are more heterogeneous than perpetrators of other subtypes in part because the pool of perpetrators is larger. However, adult children comprise the largest category, followed by other relatives, and professional (paid) caregivers (Jackson, 2016a). Both males (56%) and females are offenders, but they are not characterized by dependency. A small proportion, however, are characterized by some form of psychopathology.

The victims tend to be relatively financially and physically independent, although early forms of cognitive impairment are increasingly being implicated (Dong, Simon, Rajan, & Evans, 2011; Lichtenberg, 2016; Marson, Hebert, & Solomon, 2011). The fact that early cognitive impairments (e.g., mild cognitive impairment, executive functioning disorders) are unobservable and undiagnosed means that some vulnerable older adults moving about in the community are being exposed to potential offenders (Wood & Lichtenberg, 2017). Social isolation is frequently asserted to be a risk factor for elder abuse. However, several well-designed studies now find that larger social networks put people at risk for financial exploitation (Beach, Schulz, & Sneed, 2016; Holtfreter et al., 2014). Gender as a risk factor fails to emerge in any study using multivariate analyses, although it is likely that financial exploitation operates differently for men (e.g., theft by a paid caregiver) and women (e.g., pressure to cosign a car loan by an adult child and then the offspring fails to pay the loan). Widowhood status may act differently depending on gender as well. Nievod (1992) early on identified the major life transition of widowhood, with husbands acting as barriers to financial exploitation, and on the husband's death, the mother becomes financially vulnerable, either because she has not handled the family finances (a condition that will change in the coming decades) or because she is unable to deny her children's requests for financial assistance. Widowers, on the other hand, are susceptible to young women, some of whom are willing to exchange money for sexual favors (Jackson & Hafemeister, 2010).

A number of protective factors have been identified for financial exploitation. These include having a partner (considered a buffer against a family member's taking advantage of an older parent or grandparent), being Latino, better health (Laumann, Leitsch, & Waite, 2008), the presence of at ach, Schulz, Castle, & Rosen, 2010), and having routine freter et al., 2014).

Psychological Abuse

Psychological abuse has received the least empirical attention (Fulmer et al., 2014). Some advocates argue that psychological abuse is a component of all other subtypes. In this chapter, the term is used more conservatively as a distinct form of elder abuse. Psychological abuse is sometimes paired with verbal abuse (e.g., Gil et al., 2015) and sometimes measured separately (e.g., Oh, Kim, Martins, & Kim, 2006). Psychological abuse might include verbal assaults, insults, threats, intimidation, humiliation, and harassment; treating another person like an infant; isolating an older person from his or her family, friends, or regular activities; forced social isolation; or giving an older person the "silent treatment" (Conrad et al., 2011). Several studies found that among Asian individuals, the silent treatment is considered an extreme form of punishment that may be more emotionally devastating than physical abuse (Anetzberger, Korbin, & Tomita, 1996; Le, 1998; Moon, Tomita, & Jung-Kamei, 2002).

Little is known about the perpetrators of psychological abuse. Across several studies spouses or partners are the most frequent offenders, followed by adult children and other relatives (Jackson, 2016a). Clancy et al. (2011) also noted that offenders are both male (57%) and female and tend to be living with the victim (65%).

At this point it appears as though victims of psychological abuse have significant health issues combined with low social and financial support. Not surprisingly, then, protective factors that have been identified include older age (Beach et al., 2010; Burnes et al., 2015; Macassa et al., 2013), living alone (Mouton et al., 2004), lower education (Burnes et al., 2015), never married (Mouton et al., 2004), Latino (Laumann, Leitsch, & Waite, 2008), less than one alcoholic drink per week (Mouton et al., 2004), greater functional capacity (Burnes et al., 2015), high social support (Macassa et al., 2013), and an absence of financial strain (Macassa et al., 2013).

Sexual Abuse

Sexual abuse ranges from rape to nonconsensual inappropriate touching or taking nude photographs of an older adult. Although the sexual assault literature is expansive, especially related to children (Finkel, 2013) and women on college campuses (Fisher & Sloan, 2013), literature on the sexual abuse of older adults is minimal and primarily focuses on sexual assault in long-term care facilities (e.g., Teaster, Ramsey-Klawsnik, Abner, & Kim, 2015; see Hillman, 2017, for a discussion of sexual consent in long-term care facilities). Unfortunately, with the exception of Acierno et al. (2010), too little is known about sexual assault among older adults residing in the community, or their offenders, to draw any conclusions at this point.

Polyvictimization in Later Life

There is a growing literature on the ways in which forms of elder abuse co-occur (Gil et al., 2015; Hamby, Smith, Mitchell, & Turner, 2016; Jackson & Hafemeister, 2012b), sometimes referred to as *polyvictimization in later life*. Researchers have begun to identify risk factors associated with polyvictimization, but generally, the effects of abuse are magnified when polyvictimization is in play. Among women who experienced both verbal and physical abuse (as opposed to one or the other), Mouton et al. (2004) found that they tended to be older, never married, widowed, lived alone, ethnic minority, income less than $75,000, employed in service-sector jobs, and current smokers. Dong et al. (2011) found that Mini-Mental Status Exam (Folstein, Folstein, & McHugh, 1975) scores (a measure of cognitive impairment) were associated with an increased risk of experiencing polyvictimization, with the effect becoming stronger as the number of co-occurring forms of abuse increased. Likewise, declines in physical functioning were uniquely associated with polyvictimization (Dong et al., 2012). Conversely, Lau and Waite (2011) reported that victims with a spouse were significantly less likely to experience multiple types of abuse. This area is blossoming and more will be known in the coming years.

Community-Level Risk Factors

The research into community risk factors associated with elder abuse is scant. However, a few neighborhood-level factors have been identified. Not unexpectedly, these include high crime rates, social disorganization, lack of social resources and networks, and poverty (Cramm, van Dijk, & Nieboer, 2013; Jogerst, Dawson, Hartz, Ely, & Schweitzer, 2000; Luo & Waite, 2011; Schiamberg & Gans, 2000). Unfortunately, much more remains to be learned.

Societal-Level Risk Factors

Harbison (2016) chastised the field for focusing on individual-level factors to the near exclusion of structural and societal factors. Indeed, at the societal level elder abuse may be affected by public attitudes (Dow & Joosten, 2012), including ageism (Harbison, 2016). For example, once a person appears old, they may be perceived as stupid and incompetent (Taylor, Killick, O'Brien, Begley, & Carter-Anand, 2014). Polivka (2012) argued that changes in social policy regarding retirement bear greater responsibility for the financial harms of older adults than financial exploitation. Although frequently mentioned (e.g., Teaster et al., 2010), little empirical work has gone into validating the belief that social policies impact elder abuse. However, Lindert et al. (2013) and Macassa et al. (2013) concluded that rates of elder abuse varied by European country, suggesting the possibility that social policy embedded within these different cultures and countries in some way affects elder abuse. The "how" has yet to be empirically determined.

CONCLUSION

This review of risk factors paints a relatively distinct portrait for each type of elder abuse. Even within each type of abuse, there may be nuanced differences that quantitative data fail to capture (Daniel & Bowes, 2011; Jackson & Hafemeister, 2010). In addition, more will be learned as research becomes increasingly sophisticated, for example, taking severity of abuse into account (Burnes, Pillemer, & Lachs, 2016). Even when a particular variable is associated with multiple types of abuse (e.g., dementia; Cooper, Selwood, Blanchard, et al., 2009; Dong et al., 2014, 2011), the manifestation and impact may differ in important ways (Tronetti, 2014). Although there is increasing recognition of the importance of distinguishing among types of abuse when identifying risk factors (Jackson & Hafemeister, 2013d), the field is just beginning to understand co-occurrence as well (Hamby, Smith, Mitchell, & Turner, 2016). Unfortunately, other than compiling a list, little is known about the ebb and flow of risk factors or their interconnectedness. The absence of longitudinal research in the field is palpable. The search for modifiable risk factors upon which to base interventions will continue.

Finally, a postscript on social isolation. Social isolation is perhaps the risk factor with the longest history in this field, and yet the concept of social isolation in the context of elder abuse is vague, at best, and often conflated with related concepts (Jackson, 2015a). There are certainly situations in which a perpetrator purposefully isolates an older adult by refusing to allow friends and relatives to visit. However, a dynamic that receives much less attention occurs when a victim and perpetrator (e.g., a son with a mental illness) are cohabitating. Because of the mother's fierce protection of her son, and the son's sometimes bizarre and frightening behaviors, over time, family (including other adult children) and friends refuse to visit the older adult while the perpetrator is living in the home because they are afraid or they do not approve of the way the perpetrator is treating the older adult (Jackson & Hafemeister, 2015, 2016). Sometimes family members perceive the aging parent as having "chosen" the cohabitating child over the others and stop visiting. There are some older adults who are self-isolated, consistently having few or no friends or family throughout their lives. Finally, there are some older adults who have relatively superficial associations (e.g., they belong to a garden club) but no close friends or family that they feel they can call on in an emergency (Jackson & Hafemeister, 2010).

3

Cognitive Capacity and Communication Challenges

Cognitive capacity (decision-making ability), which is distinct from but related to *cognitive impairment* (brain functioning), forms the foundation for all subsequent actions in an elder abuse investigation and is therefore a crucial element in that context. The American Psychological Association (APA; 2014) "Guidelines for Psychological Practice With Older Adults" recommend that clinicians working with older adults be familiar with these concepts (pp. 42–44). Moreover, because older adults may have lower cognitive capacity or other mental or physical challenges, clinicians may have difficulty communicating with them. This chapter presents a brief primer on cognition and capacity, followed by recommendations for meeting the unique communication challenges of working with older adults.

http://dx.doi.org/10.1037/0000056-003
Understanding Elder Abuse: A Clinician's Guide, by S. L. Jackson

WHY COGNITIVE FUNCTIONING DECLINES

Cognition is a term used to describe many mental abilities such as decision making, memory, attention, and problem solving (Institute of Medicine [IOM], 2015). It has been long established that *fluid intelligence* (the ability to think and reason abstractly, problem solving) is age sensitive and declines with age, whereas *crystalline intelligence* (verbal ability, knowledge from previous learning or experience) is age insensitive and can be maintained and even strengthened in later life (Craik & Salthouse, 2011). Although there is tremendous variability, overall, older adults may experience declines in cognitive functioning through three mechanisms: normal cognitive aging, neurodegenerative disease such as dementia, and mild cognitive impairment.

Normal Cognitive Aging

Normal cognitive aging is a process of gradual, ongoing, yet highly variable changes in cognitive functioning (IOM, 2015). Although cognitive functioning generally declines with age, it is an individualized process.

Neurodegenerative Disease

Declines in cognitive ability may be due to neurodegenerative disease such as dementia (*Diagnostic and Statistical Manual of Mental Disorders* [5th ed.; *DSM–5*; American Psychiatric Association, 2013] uses the term *major neurocognitive disorder* rather than *dementia*; Simpson, 2014). Dementia is a syndrome caused by damage to the brain and is defined as a constellation of symptoms (not a disease), indicating a decline in cognitive functioning relative to previous higher levels of functioning (Manning & Ducharme, 2010). It is characterized by a progression of deterioration of main cognitive functions, changes in personality and social behavior, and difficulties fulfilling activities of daily living (ADLs). Memory loss is no longer a prerequisite for a diagnosis of dementia (American Psychiatric Association, 2013; Simpson, 2014). Over 100 forms of neurodegenerative dementia have been identified, although there are six primary forms, with Alzheimer's disease being the most common (Manning & Ducharme, 2010). Other relatively common dementias include

- vascular dementia,
- frontotemporal dementia,
- dementia with Lewy bodies,
- Parkinson's dementia,
- normal pressure hydrocephalus, and
- ventromedial prefrontal cortex dementia.

In 2002, the prevalence of dementia among individuals ages 71 and older was 13.9% (Plassman et al., 2007), with another 22.2% having some form of cognitive impairment without dementia (Plassman et al., 2008). The prevalence of cognitive impairment clearly increases with age (Alzheimer's Association, 2015).

Mild Cognitive Impairment

Mild cognitive impairment (MCI), sometimes conflated with dementia, is, in fact, not a form of dementia. MCI (the *DSM–5* [American Psychiatric Association, 2013] uses the term *minor neurocognitive disorder* rather than MCI; Simpson, 2014) is defined by four elements: (a) a subjective cognitive complaint, (b) objective evidence of impairment (via a battery of standardized tests), (c) normal functional activities of daily living (ADLs) and relatively intact instrumental activities of daily living (IADLs), and (d) does not meet criteria for dementia (Petersen et al., 2014). Scholars have further categorized MCI by *amnestic* (memory impairment) and *non-amnestic* (absence of memory impairment) MCI. The progression of MCI is variable, and at this time scholars are unable to predict which cases will develop into dementia (Roberts et al., 2014), but clearly not all do.

SCREENING FOR COGNITIVE FUNCTIONING

This section provides a brief review of cognitive screens and instruments to familiarize clinicians with these instruments as recommended by APA (2014, pp. 46–47). Dementia is underdiagnosed (about 55% of cases are not diagnosed), and scholars have called for screening of older adults to detect cognitive deficits (Ismail, Rajji, & Shulman, 2010; Larner, 2017). The goal of a screen is to identify cognitive deficits early, thus enabling earlier treatment regimens and environmental supports to ensure safety (Ismail et al., 2010; Mast & Gerstenecker, 2010) and reduce the negative consequences associated with unidentified cognitive impairment such as financial exploitation. In addition, a diagnosis can provide afflicted individuals and their families an explanation for the odd behavior observed and time to develop a plan to address it (Ismail et al., 2010).

In response to the need to identify cognitive deficits among older adults, over 100 cognitive screens have been developed. Many are in use in everyday practice (Dong, Chen, & Simon, 2014; see American Bar Association [ABA] Commission on Law and Aging & APA, 2008, for a list of screens; see also the National Institute on Aging at http://www.nia.nih.gov/research/cognitive-instrument/search). The Mini-Mental Status Exam (MMSE; Folstein, Folstein, & McHugh, 1975) is the most frequently used cognitive screen in clinical/health care practice and by adult protective services (APS) caseworkers (Ismail et al., 2010; Manning & Ducharme, 2010; Quinn, 2013). However, as more is learned about cognition, it is becoming increasingly evident that existing cognitive screens are inadequate (IOM, 2015). For example, the widely used MMSE is less able to identify early stages of dementia and does not capture impairments in executive functioning (a set of mental skills required for judgment and complex decision making; Ismail et al., 2010; Manning & Ducharme, 2010) and is best used to rule out dementia (Mitchell, 2009). Briefly, the newer cognitive screens have better sensitivity (correctly identify earlier stages of dementia), address executive functioning, and are less influenced by culture and education (Ismail et al., 2010). The Montreal Cognitive Assessment (MoCA; Julayanont & Nasreddine, 2017), for example, provides a measure of executive functioning, which is important for judgment and complex decision making. The U.S. Preventive Services Task Force, however, concluded that "current evidence is insufficient to assess the balance of benefits and harms of screening for cognitive impairment" (Moyer & the U.S. Preventive Services Task Force, 2014, p. 478). Although universal screening is ill-advised, the need for individual cognitive screening is unequivocal. Clinicians are reminded, however, that a cognitive screen is never a replacement for a neuropsychological assessment but simply a starting place (Larner, 2017).

COGNITIVE CAPACITY

In contrast to cognition and cognitive impairment (brain functioning), *cognitive capacity* refers to an individual's decision-making ability (i.e., the ability to understand, appreciate, manipulate information, and form a rational decision; ABA/APA, 2008; Moye & Braun, 2010). In some cases, cognitive capacity is affected by dementia, but these are not equivalent constructs (Marett & Mossman, 2015). A person may have dementia (or a psychiatric disorder) and still retain decision-making capacity (Johnson & Karlawish, 2015; Moye & Braun, 2010).

Importantly, choice is only one of the intellectual factors needed to demonstrate capable decision making (Lichtenberg, Stoltman, Ficker, Iris, & Mast, 2015). *Executional capacity*, the ability to implement a decision, is also necessary (Falk & Hoffman, 2014). Difficulties executing a decision may be related to deficits in executive functioning (Falk & Hoffman, 2014). There are a variety of influences on cognitive capacity other than neurodegenerative disease (Pinsker, Pachana, Wilson, Tilse, & Byrne, 2010; Russo, Bush, & Rasin-Waters, 2013), including relationship dynamics (O'Connor, Hall, & Donnelly, 2009). Like cognition generally, decisional capacity has been shown to undergo profound age-related changes (IOM, 2015; Tymula, Rosenberg Belmaker, Ruderman, Glimcher, & Levy, 2013). Nevertheless, a person is presumed to retain decision-making capacity unless a court has expressly determined that they lack this capacity. Russo et al. (2013), however, cautioned that an assumption of capacity does not imply optimal capacity.

Cognitive Capacity Assessment

There are multiple types of civil decision-making capacity, including financial, consent to medical treatment, research participation, testamentary capacity, sexual consent, voting, driving, and independent living (Karel,

2011). Determining cognitive capacity through a neuropsychological evaluation involves an assessment of how well an individual's functional abilities allow them to meet the requirements of a particular decision (Mast & Gerstenecker, 2010; Mosqueda & Olsen, 2015; Scheiderer, 2012; Wiglesworth, Kemp, & Mosqueda, 2008). Even if the brain structure is known, the functional capacities of the older adult cannot be fully anticipated without a neuropsychological assessment. Such an assessment might include a personal history; description of the onset, course, and nature of deficits; assessment of ADLs and IADLs; a medical record review; and administration of performance tests. There is still variability among clinicians in arriving at a capacity determination; therefore, professionals are encouraged to adopt an interdisciplinary approach to capacity assessment (Moye & Braun, 2010). Scholars also recommend avoiding assessing capacity in a vacuum because with proper supports in place, some older adults are able to exercise decision-making ability, although an assessment of the individual in isolation might indicate otherwise (Lichtenberg et al., 2015; Pinsker et al., 2010). Capacity may fluctuate throughout the day, and, as such, an older adult may be better able to provide consent or perform better on different days or at different times of the day (Little, Satlin, Sunderland, & Volicer, 1995). Older adults know when they function most optimally, and clinicians involved in assessing capacity are encouraged to ask their clients for this information.

It is important to note that a person can refuse to consent to a capacity assessment (Russo et al., 2013). This refusal is allowed because an assessment of capacity that finds a person incapacitated can result in loss of significant civil rights (Moye & Braun, 2010). As noted, older adults with diminished capacity in one or more areas may still retain capacity in other areas. Courts are increasingly recognizing this fact when guardianship is implicated, and hence courts are limiting loss of rights to designated areas, referred to as *limited guardianship* (Moye, Butz, Marson, Wood, & ABA/APA, 2007).

Financial Capacity

Financial management becomes increasingly complex throughout the lifespan, at the same time that financial decision making becomes increasingly compromised (Hershey, Austin, & Gutierrez, 2015). Successful aging is based on independence (i.e., choice), and independence is based on financial security, which can be threatened when an individual has diminished financial capacity (Lichtenberg, 2016; Pinsker et al., 2010). The older adult with diminished financial capacity may be more vulnerable to their own financial errors as well as to financial exploitation (and scams) by others. Therefore, one specific type of civil capacity that has received considerable attention in the past decade is *financial capacity*. It is defined as the ability to manage one's financial affairs in a manner that is consistent with self-interest and personal values (Marson, Hebert, & Solomon, 2011). Financial capacity comprises a broad range of conceptual, pragmatic, and judgment abilities, ranging from basic skills, such as counting coins, to more complex skills, such as paying bills and managing a checkbook (Marson et al., 2000).

Different forms of dementia have different underlying processes and pathologies, which affect different aspects of capacity (Pinsker et al., 2010). As with capacity generally, financial capacity might be influenced by a host of factors, including depression, anxiety, psychosis, psychiatric symptoms, social networks, traditional gender roles, imbalance of power in relationships, and culture (Pinsker et al., 2010). However, older adults with dementia or even MCI are more likely to have diminished financial capacity compared with controls (Marson et al., 2000). Clinicians may want to learn whether an older client is receiving financial management assistance; however, it is important to realize that receipt of financial management assistance by family members (referred to as *family financial caregiving*) is not indicative of cognitive dysfunction. Older adults receive assistance with financial management far more frequently for reasons other than dementia, such as inexperience or loss of interest (Gillen & Kim, 2014).

Financial capacity appears to deteriorate sooner than other IADLs, and well before ADLs (Marson et al., 2000). Scientists warn that diminished financial capacity is not readily observable and therefore can go undetected (Flint, Sudore, & Widera, 2012). In addition, older adults fail to recognize their own financial capacity deficits (Van Wielingen, Tuokko, Cramer, Mateer, & Hultsch, 2004) and subjectively rate their financial abilities higher than their performance on an objective measure (Okonkwo

nermore, older adults may be the least likely to sus-
ing financially exploited (Bagshaw, Wendt, Zannettino,
3), especially when it involves a family member (Knight
).

mismatch between actual and perceived financial capacity helps
to explain the prevalence of financial exploitation perpetrated against
older adults but suggests that education and warnings alone may not be
sufficient to prevent financial exploitation (Barnard, 2009). Determining the point at which a cognitively impaired older adult is no longer
capable of independent financial management is challenging, and there
is no agreed-on point of intervention (Pinsker et al., 2010). It also may
be more difficult for APS caseworkers to make a disposition of financial
exploitation when the victim has full mental capacity. Indeed, the presence of cognitive deficits is more likely than the nature of the financial
offense itself (e.g., misuse of a power of attorney, theft) to move social
workers and health care professionals to intervene in a financial exploitation case (Davies, Gilhooly, Gilhooly, Harries, & Cairns, 2013).

The foundation of a financial capacity assessment is a *capacity assessment* (Moye & Braun, 2010; see ABA/APA, 2008), typically encompassing
nine domains:

- legal standard,
- functional elements,
- diagnosis,
- cognitive underpinnings,
- psychiatric or emotional factors,
- values,
- risk considerations,
- steps to enhance capacity, and
- clinical judgment of capacity.

However, in the context of financial capacity, these nine domains
are assessed as they relate to financial skills and judgment (Marson et al.,
2000). The focus of financial capacity assessments is on how cognitive
deficits impair financial functioning after other possible causes have been

excluded, such as social and cultural factors, factors the the performance-based assessment (Pinsker et al., 2(cial decision-making screens are under development ⎣ 2016).

COMMUNICATING WITH OLDER ADULTS

Because of cognitive impairment and other challenges, clinicians may encounter obstacles in communicating with older adults. Not all clinicians are familiar with the nuances involved in communicating with "older adults" (APA, 2014; Baladerian & Heisler, 2010; Payne & Berg, 2003), a category that can include up to three generations (Wenger, 2002). Some accommodations may be necessary (APA, 2014; Cook & Niederehe, 2007). For example, communicating with older adults may require

- more time;
- frequent breaks, as older adults may find sitting for long periods of time difficult; or
- scheduling visits around routines or peak performance times.

When determining whether accommodations are necessary, clinicians should consider whether there are sensory impairments, cognitive impairments, or cultural considerations with older adults.

Sensory Impairments

Some older adults may have sensory impairments that require special consideration (see Gerontological Society of America, 2011, for practical tips on interviewing older adults). However, do not assume impairments are present, but instead ask older adults in a sensitive manner whether they have such impairments.

- Hearing impairments: If the older adult is hearing impaired, acknowledge this and explain that you will speak clearly. Explain that you will take the time necessary to be sure the older adult understands the question. Sit face-to-face with the older adult as sometimes facial features and lip reading help with hearing impairments (Wenger, 2002).

- Vision impairments: Having a vision impairment does not interfere with comprehension. However, relationship building is facilitated when the interviewer sits close enough to the older adult to allow them to clearly see your face (if culturally appropriate; Beerman & Markarian, 2004). Older adults may need assistance with reading materials because of vision or literacy limitations.
- Speech impairments: Older adults with speech impairments can be interviewed, but it may require patience. Bear in mind that people with speech impairments (e.g., resulting from a stroke) tire quickly from the effort of speaking (Wenger, 2002).

Cognitive Impairments

The presence of a cognitive impairment does not unequivocally mean that an older adult cannot participate in an interview. Never assume the presence or absence of a cognitive impairment. Clinicians must be aware that social skills and speech may be perfectly intact, although a cognitive impairment may be present. Conversely, communication that seems incongruous does not necessarily mean that the person has a cognitive impairment (Wenger, 2002). De Vries (2013) and Mosqueda (2013) provided more practical guidance on communicating with this population.

Cultural Sensitivity

As with all interviews, clinicians must be sensitive to cultural differences among clients (Wenger, 2002). Consider, for example, gender beliefs, filial responsibilities, and age-related historical experiences. Communication should be conducted in the interviewee's first language, which in some cases requires the use of translators other than family members (Office for Victims of Crime, 2011).

CONCLUSION

Clinicians with a working knowledge of the constructs of cognition and cognitive capacity (including financial capacity) will have a better understanding of the strengths and weaknesses of their clients, as well as their clients' legal and ethical rights discussed in subsequent chapters. Depending on these and other factors, clinicians may need to adjust the way they communicate with older adults. Simple adjustments in communication can add clarity as well as signal respect to the older adult.

4

Detection and Legal Obligations to Report

The previous chapters aimed to familiarize clinicians with the field of elder abuse. Such foundational information enables clinicians to detect elder abuse. This chapter describes the actual process of detection in part by describing how various groups perceive and characterize elder abuse. Detection may be enhanced with the use of elder abuse screens, also reviewed in this chapter. Detection in some states triggers a reporting obligation for clinicians; therefore, a thorough discussion of mandatory reporting laws and associated rights and responsibilities is provided.

DETECTING ELDER ABUSE

As described in Chapter 2, the field has focused on the identification of risk factors to increase clinicians' ability to detect—and ultimately report—elder abuse to ensure that older adults are made aware of various available

http://dx.doi.org/10.1037/0000056-004
Understanding Elder Abuse: A Clinician's Guide, by S. L. Jackson

services. Studies have found that for every reported case of elder abuse, up to 24 cases go unreported (Lachs & Berman, 2011), in part because of the difficulty in detecting abuse in the first place (Cooper, Selwood, & Livingston, 2008). Unsurprisingly, efforts are often made to conceal the occurrence of elder abuse, and it may be difficult even for those who regularly interact with an older adult to detect an abusive situation (Brandl et al., 2007). Detection may be obfuscated by an older individual's reluctance to discuss the matter, assist with an investigation, or acknowledge that abuse occurred (Schmeidel, Daly, Rosenbaum, Schmuch, & Jogerst, 2012). Detection is all the more difficult when older adults are isolated and there are no individuals with whom they routinely interact (Reeves & Wysong, 2010; Wilber & Reynolds, 1997).

Detection is also hampered because people differ in what they believe constitutes abuse (Davies et al., 2011; Penhale, 2010) or there may be alternative explanations for suspicious behavior (e.g., the physical injury was the result of an accidental fall, the transfer of assets was an intended gift; Scheiderer, 2012). Furthermore, the ability to detect elder abuse may vary with the type of abuse involved. Conrad et al. (2011) argued that psychological abuse is the most difficult form of elder abuse to detect, while others have argued that financial exploitation and neglect are harder to detect (Davies, Gilhooly, Gilhooly, Harries, & Cairns, 2013; Schmeidel et al., 2012).

There are a variety of individuals who might be in a position to detect elder abuse (Brandl et al., 2007). These individuals include neighbors and friends (Barker, 2002), professionals such as health care providers (Cooper, Selwood, & Livingston, 2009; Davies et al., 2013; Kennedy, 2005; Schmeidel et al., 2012), employees of financial institutions (Snyder, 2012), lawyers (Dessin, 2005), adult protective services (APS) caseworkers (Davies et al., 2011), and psychologists and other mental health providers (Roberto, 2016; Zeranski & Halgin, 2011). Family members are also in a position to detect elder abuse and facilitate intervention (Beidler, 2012). In some cases, family members may be unaware of the abuse or be alerted to the situation by an emerging crisis and then promptly respond. However, there are times when family members have been aware of ongoing abuse and for various reasons have long refrained from taking action (Breckman & Adelman, 1988; Jackson & Hafemeister, 2015).

CONCEPTUALIZATION OF ELDER ABUSE

A behavior must reach some threshold to be identified as abuse, a thres old that varies among individuals in part depending on how they conceptualize elder abuse. There are some important differences in the way groups of individuals conceptualize elder abuse.

Older Adults in the General Public

Little is known about the general public's knowledge and perceptions of elder abuse (Lindland, Fond, Haydon, & Kendall-Taylor, 2015). However, the general public may have misperceptions based in part on media coverage, which may be distorted (Mastin, Choi, Barboza, & Post, 2007). Some nonabused older adults view older abuse victims as an "other" category, suggesting that elder abuse is something that happens to other older people (Naughton, Drennan, & Lafferty, 2014).

However, among older adults there is general recognition of the concept of elder abuse (Naughton et al., 2014; Taylor, Killick, O'Brien, Begley, & Carter-Anand, 2014). Studies have found that when asked, older adults are most frequently able to identify psychological abuse (Naughton et al., 2014), followed by caregiver neglect, with greater variability for physical abuse and financial exploitation. Participants generally fail to identify sexual abuse, but when prompted, they agree that it happens, for example, "You hear about it, you read it in the paper." These studies suggest that certain types of abuse are more widely recognized than others. However, not all older adults can identify elder abuse. A study in the United Kingdom revealed that despite 2 years of public education campaigns, the messages were not reaching the less educated and oldest–old who were in poor health and residing in deprived communities—individuals who may be at higher risk for abuse (Acierno et al., 2010; Naughton et al., 2012; O'Keeffe et al., 2007).

Differences by Victim Characteristics

Characteristics associated with the victim might influence whether behaviors are viewed as abusive. Mouton et al. (2005) reported that older people who

or mental capacity were deemed by participants to
herefore the actions of the caregiver were perceived
ely, an older person who seems to have the capacity
quences of exploitation, but chooses to remain in the
be viewed as abused (Doerner & Lab, 2015).

Differences by Victim–Abuser Relationship

As distinguished from denial (e.g., Enguidanos, DeLiema, Aguilar, Lambrinos, & Wilber, 2014), older adults may differ in their conceptualization of abuse based on relationship status. For example, older adults are less likely to perceive an action as financial exploitation when the exploiter is an offspring versus a paid caregiver or a more distant relative (Knight et al., 2016). Conversely, what might be considered abusive in the formal (paid) caregiving context would not be considered abusive in the family caregiving context (Taylor et al., 2014), perhaps in part because professional staff should know better (Mouton et al., 2005).

Differences in Abuser's Intent

Relatedly, the intent of the abuser seems to play a particular role in perceptions of neglect. For example, Taylor et al. (2014) found that participants perceived it acceptable for the caregiver of a family member with Alzheimer's disease to bolt the doors shut while the caregiver went out for 5 or 10 minutes to calm down or pick up milk. Perceived as unacceptable, however, was a caregiver who kept the family member with Alzheimer's disease at home without support, rather than placing the family member in a long-term care facility, in an effort to preserve the older adult's finances to pad the caregiver's inheritance. Relatively similar actions, but diametrically opposed intentions, influenced the acceptability of the action.

Differences in Offense Characteristics

Aspects of the offense also might influence judgments about elder abuse. For example, Mouton et al. (2005) found that older adults perceived habitual abuse as more serious than a single event. It may be that after many years of abuse, victims themselves begin to accept violent behavior as "normal" (Band-Winterstein, Avieli, & Smeloy, 2016), and therefore they are less likely to label the act as abusive. The nature of the offense also might influence these judgments. In describing an Australian report (D'Aurizio, 2007), Mihaljcic and Lowndes (2013) conveyed that the majority of participants in that study rated as "extremely serious" pressuring an older person to withdraw money from their bank account against their will and receiving a government benefit to care for an older person and not providing care. In contrast, only half of the participants rated as "extremely serious" a family member, friend, or caregiver who insisted on living with an older person but did not pay for the accommodation or contribute toward bills.

Differences Between Victims and Professionals

Taylor et al. (2014) cogently pointed out that the same actions viewed by victims may be viewed differently by others, including professionals (Eisikovits, Koren, & Band-Winterstein, 2013; Helmes & Cuevas, 2007; Jackson & Hafemeister, 2013a; Mihaljcic & Lowndes, 2013). For example, a son who visits his mother each week and "takes" $50 may not be perceived by the mother as financially abusive. Her son is coming to visit her, and there is an underlying right or unspoken agreement between the two about finances. However, professionals may perceive this as financial exploitation.

Also in the context of financial exploitation, Mihaljcic and Lowndes (2013) found differences between older adults and professionals with regard to the abusive acts, the abusive individuals, the causes of abuse, and the possible solutions. For example, older adults opined that when they lent money to their children, they rarely expected the money to be repaid with interest, or at all, whereas aged care workers considered borrowing money from an older adult as financially abusive when the money or assets were no longer available to the older adult or not returned as soon as the money or asset was needed. In contrast, likely because older adults fail to label the actions of family members as abusive (Knight et al.,

2016), older adults perceived financial institutions as the most likely "abusers," whereas aged care professionals viewed family members as the most likely abusers. Older adults identified the cause of elder abuse to be related to a lack of education or experience with money management, particularly for women, and that children frequently believe older people do not need money and therefore should help them financially. In contrast, aged care workers identified older adults' vulnerability as the cause of elder abuse primarily because of their medical problems, dementia, and family dynamics. Because the issue is framed differently for each group, their solutions also differed. Older adults in the study identified education as the best preventive measure, whereas aging care professionals identified the need for greater professional and formal regulations. These differences in perceptions interfere with the clinician's ability to effectively intervene (Jackson & Hafemeister, 2013a).

Professionals and victims also may focus on different aspects of the elder abuse situation. The emotional aspects of all types of abuse may be difficult for professionals to detect, whereas bruising as a sign of physical abuse may be more easily recognized. However, in focus groups, older adults gave psychological aspects of abuse the greatest weight, suggesting that increased attention to emotional aspects of abuse is critically important to victims but will require higher levels of professional skill to detect it (Taylor et al., 2014).

Culture

There are different social, familial, and generational expectations and attitudes regarding appropriate behavior within families that may differ across cultures (Mihaljcic & Lowndes, 2013; Taylor et al., 2014). Distinct ethnic or racial groups may perceive the experience of abuse differently (Lee, Kaplan, & Perez-Stable, 2014) and experience elder abuse in different ways (Enguidanos et al., 2014) and even at different rates (Flores, Burnett, Booker, & Dyer, 2015). Alaskan Native and Native American cultures embrace the family, tribal unity, and interdependence (Jervis, Fickenscher, Beals, & the Shielding American Indian Elders Project Team, 2014). Chang and Moon (1997) found that older Korean Americans' understanding of abuse was based on Korean cultural

norms relating primarily to parent–child relat.
and the responsibilities of adult children towa.
Tomita, & Jung-Kamei, 2002). However, compared \
or Caucasian American women, older Korean Americ.
likely to perceive a set of scenarios as abusive (Moon & W
another small study of older adults and their caregivers acr.
groups, Anetzberger, Korbin, and Tomita (1996) found that si.   .ngs
in performing the caring role was one of the most egregious act. .ommit-
ted by a family member. However, African American and Japanese American individuals were significantly more likely to perceive such behavior as
abusive than were Caucasian and Puerto Rican individuals.

Summary

Clinicians may not be able to rely on older adults' voluntary disclosure
of abuse. Clinicians must recognize that how older adults and clinicians
perceive elder abuse may differ, with some older adults failing to recognize
or label actions as abusive. Therefore, it is incumbent upon clinicians to
inquire specifically about elder abuse if there is at least some suspicion
of abuse. If a disclosure is not forthcoming, clinicians may want to use
screening instruments.

SCREENING FOR ELDER ABUSE AS A FORM OF DETECTION

Elder abuse is sometimes detected through screening, although it is unknown
how widely screening is practiced. Screening instruments are designed to
be administered quickly to identify individuals who may be victims of or
at risk of abuse. Screens are not a diagnosis of abuse, but they do provide a
warning to engage in additional assessment (Cohen, Halevi-Levin, Gagin,
& Friedman, 2006).

The American Psychological Association (APA; 2014) "Guidelines for
Psychological Practice With Older Adults" recommend that clinicians be
familiar with the tools used with older adults (pp. 46–47). Existing elder
abuse screens (as opposed to cognitive screens) may be completed by either

tioners or cognitively intact older adults (see Wiglesworth et al., 2010, for possible screening questions for people with dementia). Reviews of existing instruments, however, generally have found them psychometrically deficient in some manner (Burnett, Achenbaum, & Murphy, 2014; Cohen, 2011; Fulmer, Guadagno, Dyer, & Connolly, 2004; Imbody & Vandsburger, 2011; Moore & Browne, 2016; Pisani & Walsh, 2012). The following are brief descriptions of the six predominant elder abuse screens (excluding screens administered to caregivers):

- Elder Abuse Suspicion Index (EASI; Yaffe, Wolfson, Lithwick, & Weiss, 2008). Developed by and for physicians, the six-item EASI is administered by a professional (although it has been used as a self-report) and takes 2 minutes to administer (Item 6 is completed by the physician/clinician). Although it does identify types of elder abuse, the low sensitivity means that there will be a high number of false negatives, necessitating clinical follow-up.
- Brief Abuse Screen for the Elderly (BASE; Reis & Nahmiash, 1995). Administered by a professional, the six-item BASE takes one minute to administer but is predicated on extensive training in elder abuse.
- Hwalek-Sengstock Elder Abuse Screening Test (H-S/EAST; Neale, Hwalek, Scott, Sengstock, & Stahl, 1991). Typically administered by a professional, the six-item H-S/EAST is quick and easy to administer (taking 3 minutes), but it assesses for dependency, coercion, and vulnerability rather than types of abuse. The screen has high false negatives, and the coercion variable is unstable.
- Vulnerability to Abuse Screening Scale (VASS; Schofield & Mishra, 2003). The VASS is remarkably similar to the H-S/EAST but was created to assess for abuse among older women. It is likewise quick and easy to administer (either by a professional or as self-report), but it is less well vetted in terms of psychometrics.
- Elder Assessment Instrument (EAI; Fulmer, Paveza, Abraham, & Fairchild, 2000). The 41-item EAI functions as a clinical checklist rather than a screen, taking 15 minutes to complete. In addition to taking longer to complete, it relies heavily on clinical judgment.

- Indicators of Abuse (IOA; Reis & Nahmiash, 1998; Cohen et ∖
  The 27-item IOA functions as an indicator of risk rather than ∖
  abuse screen. It is part of a 2- to 3-hour clinical interview desig.
  alert the clinician to the possibility of abuse depending on the score. As
  it is an unstandardized instrument, practitioners may produce diverse
  results due to differences in interviewing and diagnostic skills. The
  measure does not capture financial exploitation.

Screens are predicated on the principle of *beneficence*, the idea that
they do more good than harm. The U.S. Preventive Services Task Force,
however, found no valid and reliable screening tools to identify abuse of
older or vulnerable adults in the primary care setting. Therefore, they
could not recommend universal screening because of a lack of knowledge
with regard to the risks and benefits of such screening and because the
effectiveness of interventions is unclear at this time (Moyer & the U.S. Preventive Services Task Force, 2013), a claim recently echoed by Moore and
Browne (2016). Because there is no perfected screening instrument, clinicians are advised to use an elder abuse screen (or indicators of abuse; see
also Mosqueda & Olsen, 2015, p. 679, for possible screening questions) as
part of a holistic assessment, including the use of their clinical judgment,
rather than relying exclusively on one screen or another.

During the screening process, clinicians must be sensitive because
for some older adults, the person abusing them is someone they care for
deeply, and denigrating the offender will only raise their defenses. Clinicians are urged to convey the purpose of the screen, normalize the process, avoid blaming statements, reiterate confidentiality limitations, and
assure clients that they can refuse to answer any questions. Adapted from
Henderson, Varble, and Buchanan (2004, p. 754), the clinician might begin
with the following:

> Mr. B, I am going to ask you a set of questions that I ask every client
> who is age 60 and older [depending on the requirements in your state]
> to see if you are experiencing any problems with the people in your
> life who might be abusive or neglectful or inappropriately using your
> money. I make it a policy to ask all of my older clients because it is

more common than most people think, and if you are experiencing some problems with a family member or someone you care about I'd like to be able to do something to help. We talked at our first session about my limits to confidentiality—that there are certain actions that I am legally required to report—one of them being elder abuse. If, after I ask you these questions, I suspect you are being mistreated by another person, I am legally bound to make a report to APS. In my state, elder abuse is defined as. . . . Please be aware that you are perfectly free to decline to answer my questions, but I encourage you to answer them honestly so I can get you the help you need—if in fact you need help.

If the older client is in immediate danger, never send them home to a dangerous situation (Henderson et al., 2004). Clinicians are urged to immediately contact APS in the client's jurisdiction. In all instances, careful documentation of the screening and the conclusion is necessary. This information may be used later to support a claim of elder abuse. Records should be completed in a way that will allow their admissibility in court.

FORENSIC MARKERS AS TRIGGERS FOR DETECTION

Detection has been seriously undermined by the absence of forensic markers that helped propel the child abuse field (Parton, 1979). With few exceptions (Ziminski, Wiglesworth, Austin, Phillips, & Mosqueda, 2013), the field of elder abuse suffers from a lack of forensic markers, hampering the ability of geriatricians and other health care providers to differentiate between aging and abusive behavior (LoFaso & Rosen, 2014), especially when victims are reluctant to disclose. The difference between accidental death and elder homicide is likewise problematic (Collins & Presnell, 2006). Because older adults bruise easily, it is challenging to determine whether a bruise resulted from abuse. In some of the only forensic bruising research available, Mosqueda, Burnight, and Liao (2005) concluded that bruising associated with elder abuse occurs more frequently on the extremities, and in contrast to what is commonly believed, color alone cannot predict the age of the bruise. Forensic science is growing and is also being applied in the context of financial exploitation, with the utilization of forensic accountants in financial exploitation investigations (S. Wood & Lichtenberg, 2017).

THE ABYSS BETWEEN DETECTION AND REPORTING

The assumption underlying efforts to increase detection is that once a victim is detected, the case will be reported and services provided. This assumption may be faulty, however, as detection and reporting are related but discrete actions (Jackson & Hafemeister, 2015). Detection requires an awareness of an abusive situation, whereas the decision to report involves a complex calculation and an affirmative action. There are many reasons why older adults and those around them choose not to report.

WHY PEOPLE CHOOSE NOT TO REPORT

Victims, family and friends, professionals, and the general public are unlikely to report elder abuse for a variety of reasons. Similar to many victims of crime (Truman & Langton, 2014), it is generally accepted that older adults are unlikely to self-report the experience of elder abuse (Teaster et al., 2006). Lachs and Berman (2011), for example, found that 17.6% of older adults self-reported abuse, a rate higher than other studies have found (Teaster et al., 2006). However, data from the National Crime Victimization Survey found that older victims were more likely to report violent victimization to police than younger (12- to 24-year-old) victims (Morgan & Mason, 2014). There are important differences across the lifespan in rates and reasons for calling law enforcement (Kang & Lynch, 2014). Furthermore, self-reporting appears to be influenced by the victim–offender relationship. Older adults are more likely to report when the quality of their relationship with the family offender is weaker (Gibson, 2013; Jackson & Hafemeister, 2015) or when the offender is a stranger (Brank, Wylie, & Hamm, 2011; Holtfreter, Reisig, Mears, & Wolfe, 2014).

Brank et al. (2011) concluded that older adults do understand that abuse is morally and legally wrong, but they choose not to report for legitimate reasons—not necessarily because of incapacity or inability, as is often assumed. Victims may not report because they

- do not want to get their loved ones in trouble (Beaulaurier, Seff, Newman, & Dunlop, 2005);
- do not want to set into motion a series of unwanted interventions, such as institutionalization (Beaulaurier, Seff, Newman, & Dunlop, 2007; Wright, 2010);
- feel they have a strong relationship with the abuser (Gibson, 2013);
- believe their situation is a family matter (Podnieks, 1992);
- do not define the behavior as abusive as in some cases of financial exploitation (Conrad, Iris, Ridings, Langley, & Wilber, 2010);
- fear retaliation from the offender;
- feel shame and embarrassment;
- do not know whom to contact for help (Beaulaurier et al., 2007);
- do not consider the case serious enough to report (Podnieks, 1992);
- do not think law enforcement will believe them (McCart, Smith, & Sawyer, 2010); and/or
- are unaware that they are being financially exploited (Jackson & Hafemeister, 2014).

Finally, some older adults disclose an abusive situation to an informal source of support (Brank et al., 2011; Breckman & Adelman, 1988; Comijs, Pot, Smit, Bouter, & Jonker, 1998; Jackson & Hafemeister, 2015), who in turn places a report with APS, a fact masked by official statistics.

Family members may not report because they are disengaged from the parent or relative, believe there is nothing they can do, are unaware of whom to contact, or have tried to intervene in the past and failed (Breckman & Adelman, 1988; Jackson & Hafemeister, 2015). The victim–offender alliance results in other family members stepping aside or being squeezed out (Breckman & Adelman, 1988). Others may perceive the victim as complicit and culpable and rationalize, "It's his/her life." However, many of these cases eventually are reported (by the victim, family members, or others) on reaching a certain threshold—generally, some level of fear for the victim's safety (Jackson & Hafemeister, 2015).

Perhaps the category most analogous to mental health clinicians is health care providers. Health care providers may not report abuse for a number of reasons. They may think they are violating patient confidentiality (Kennedy, 2005), do not ask about or recognize the signs (Kennedy, 2005), do not know whom to contact (Marson et al., 2009; Mills et al., 2012), are unlikely to perceive abuse if they believe reporting violates their patients' autonomy (Helmes & Cuevas, 2007) or believe it is not in the best interest of the older patient to be isolated from family members (Lowndes, Darzins, Wainer, Owada, & Mihaljcic, 2009). Furthermore, professionals' suspicions may not rise to the level of certainty, and they do not want to falsely accuse someone (Schmeidel et al., 2012). These professionals, in particular, may believe that someone else will or should be detecting and reporting elder abuse, notwithstanding that they know they are a mandated reporter (Schmeidel et al., 2012). Another reporting impediment is a general cynical belief that authorities charged with responding to these reports (e.g., APS caseworkers) will either fail to act or will not intervene effectively, ultimately making the situation worse (DeLiema, Navarro, Enguidanos, & Wilber, 2015; Kennedy, 2005). Although there is no research to confirm this, clinicians may have similar concerns.

Finally, members of the general public do not report because they fail to recognize elder abuse (Lindland et al., 2015), think there is nothing they can do, do not know whom to contact for help, do not want to get involved, or believe that most older adults would report the abuse themselves if they felt they needed or wanted help (Plaisance, 2008).

This review confirms that underreporting is the norm (Lachs & Berman, 2011). Therefore, clinicians cannot rely on older adults or other categories of persons to report elder abuse. If clinicians find themselves in a situation where they need to place a report, understanding older adults' concerns and beliefs about reporting, and those around them, will facilitate the clinician's ability to engage in a sensitive discussion about reporting.

ꟼLACING A REPORT OF ELDER ABUSE

Voluntary or Permissive Reporting

Anyᴗ_ can make a voluntary report. States may attempt to enhance voluntary reporting of suspected abuse by the general public by implementing public awareness campaigns. Approximately half of reports to APS originate from voluntary sources, including older victims (Teaster et al., 2006; Thomson et al., 2011). Clinicians who practice in states without a mandatory reporting law may voluntarily report but are advised to notify the older adult of their intentions and involve them in the reporting process to the extent it is feasible.

Mandatory Reporting

Because self-reports of abuse are infrequent (Teaster et al., 2006), the policy solution embraced by most authorities seeking to enhance the identification of elder abuse has been mandatory reporting, permitted under the state's exercise of the *parens patriae* authority (Kapp, 1995). In most states, the designated authority for placing reports is with (some form of) APS (e.g., Va. Code Ann., 2017a).

Mandatory reporting requires various designated groups of individuals believed to be well-positioned to detect elder abuse to relay reasonable suspicions of such abuse to designated agencies (i.e., APS or law enforcement). The underlying assumption is that those who are in a position to detect elder abuse should be required to file a report when they suspect its occurrence (Glick, 2005). With the exception of New York, all states and the District of Columbia have provisions for mandatory elder abuse reporting, although the specific provisions and the mandated reporters vary from state to state (Jirik & Sanders, 2014).

Mandatory reporting is one of the most controversial policies in the field of elder abuse. Some scholars claim that mandatory reporting laws are egregiously paternalistic (Brank et al., 2011; Glick, 2005; Kohn, 2014), although it continues to hold political prominence in our response to elder abuse, as evidenced by its nearly universal adoption by states. Such laws have been criticized for denying older adults the right to keep private and

confidential their conversations with their doctc
or other valued persons (Kohn, 2010). In additic
interventions flowing from a report are so limit
a report results in an unintended but nonethe'
the older victim (e.g., institutionalization). Ausu.
erately has no mandatory reporting law for elder abuse occui.. ɕ
community at the behest of their older population (Kurrle, 2013). However, the justification for mandatory reporting in the United States is that older adults with capacity may in every state refuse services.

Unfortunately, there is little evidence to demonstrate that mandatory reporting laws have had the intended effect of curbing the mistreatment of older Americans (Glick, 2005). It has been argued that requiring the involvement of an outside third party without the consent of the older adult, or even over the objection of the older adult in carefully defined situations, undermines the older person's autonomy (Glick, 2005). Brank et al. (2011) quipped that mandatory reporting laws are more beneficial to social services in justifying their funding than to older adults.

WHO IS OBLIGATED TO REPORT?

The mandatory reporting statutes for elder abuse encompass a fairly wide variety of potential reporters. However, all of the states that have mandatory reporting statutes require physicians or other health care providers to report elder abuse for the reason that most older people tend to visit physicians frequently and regularly (Victor, 2005). Still relatively unique is a state's statutory mandate that employees of financial institutions report suspected financial exploitation of an older adult, although this trend is growing (Bessolo, 2007). Some states also require reports by caregivers, law enforcement officers, clergy (Moskowitz & DeBoer, 1999), and most recently, lawyers (Dessin, 2005). The broadest type of mandatory reporting statute, currently utilized by 16 states, requires anyone who suspects abuse to report it. Several state statutes include the qualification that potential reporters (e.g., physicians) are only mandated to report abuse if they are acting in their official capacity or performing professional duties when it comes to their attention (e.g., Hawaii Revised Statutes, 2017). In many when the reporters are not acting in such a capacity, they may report abuse, but they are not mandated to do so.

Clinicians' Obligation to Report

There are times when a clinician's obligation to protect client information conflicts with their obligation to the state to protect older adults. One of the guiding principles for clinicians is confidentiality designed in part to promote a therapeutic alliance. However, clinicians are cognizant that there are exceptions to confidentiality both in law (e.g., *Tarasoff v. Regents of the University of California*, 1976; mandatory reporting statutes) and in ethical guidelines. The APA (2014) "Guidelines for Psychological Practice With Older Adults" provide that "in most states, practitioners are legally obligated to report suspected [elder] abuse and neglect to appropriate authorities" (p. 54), which in most states is APS. Psychologists are frequently identified in elder abuse statutes as mandated reporters (Zeranski & Halgin, 2011). State statutes vary considerably, however, and therefore clinicians must determine their state's reporting obligations (find your state's mandatory reporting law at https://www.justice.gov/elderjustice/elder-justice-statutes-0#SL3). Clinicians are ethically bound to convey to their clients the circumstances under which they are required to report in accordance with the APA's (2017) *Ethical Principles of Psychologists and Code of Conduct* (p. 7). Reporting obligations should be conveyed to potential clients at the first session to avoid misunderstanding.

Negotiating the obligation to report elder abuse while preserving the therapeutic relationship is challenging and requires forethought. Once a relationship has been established and the occurrence of elder abuse learned, it is perhaps most important to remind clients of the obligation to report and involve them in the reporting process to the greatest extent feasible, either offering to assist them in placing a report or obtaining their consent to place the report. If consent is not obtained from clients, it is still preferable to take an approach based on information and explanations of ethical and legal obligations. If the situation involves clients who are harming or threatening to harm an older adult, reasonable care to protect the victim (triggered by *Tarasoff*) must be taken and could be satisfied by a report to APS. As noted above, reasons for breaching cо should be recorded in the client's record. Finally, if the abuse is о in the context of a forensic evaluation, Glancy et al. (2015) recomm. that prior to placing the report, clinicians consult with supervisors, pee. or an attorney and discuss the potential breach of confidentiality (p. S7).

WHO IS ACTUALLY REPORTING ELDER ABUSE?

A national survey of states' APS determined that the most common source of reports were from family members (17.0%), followed by social services workers (10.6%), friends and neighbors (8.0%), and the victims themselves (6.3%; Teaster et al., 2006). More recently, Lachs and Berman (2011) found that among nonmandatory reports submitted to APS, victims self-reported in 17.6% of the cases and family members provided 14.0% of these reports, while law enforcement personnel were the most frequent group of mandated reporters to report an incident to APS (22.1%). Physicians rarely report to APS, with less than 2.0% of reports originating from physicians (Teaster et al., 2006).

WHAT KIND OF VICTIM TRIGGERS REPORTING?

Statutes define the characteristics of a victim who can be the subject of a report, and they vary widely in this respect (Jackson, 2015b). However, typically there are four categories (with variability within each category). First, some states, such as California, define an older adult by age alone (California Codes Annotated, 2017), which is perceived by some as ageist. Second, some states avoid age altogether by requiring reporting for a class of victims called *vulnerable adults*. For example, Vermont defines a vulnerable adult as any person age 18 years or older who meets any number of criteria, including being a resident of a facility; having a physical, mental, or developmental disability; or being a recipient of personal care services from a home health agency (Vermont Statutes Annotated, 2016). Third, some states use an age-and-vulnerability classification scheme, requiring not only some minimum age but also an accompanying defined vulnerability (Florida Annotated Statutes, 2017). Finally, there are a handful of states that place no limits on the characteristics that constitute a victim. As each state is different, it is imperative that practitioners know their own state's statute.

WHAT LEVEL OF CERTAINTY IS REQUIRED?

There is also considerable variance in the level of certainty required to trigger the duty to report. Some states have a very high standard of certainty. In Hawaii, for example, a reporter must have knowledge or belief that an adult has been abused or will be abused. Many states, however, have a much lower standard of certainty, often requiring only suspicion or a cause to suspect that the abuse has occurred. Many states employ a reasonableness standard, mandating a report only when the belief or suspicion is reasonable. Finally, a few states use a "reasonable person" standard, under which the reporter must decide whether a reasonable person in the same circumstances and with the same knowledge would believe that abuse was occurring or would occur. This standard can be problematic for reporters because it is difficult to characterize a "reasonable person," and this standard could be read broadly or narrowly depending on the reporter's own inclinations. As each state is different, practitioners must know their own state's statute.

WHAT INFORMATION MUST BE REPORTED?

When placing a report with APS (see Chapter 5), the clinician will typically be asked to provide the victim's age, identity, location of the incident, and the circumstances causing the concern. Reports always may be made anonymously.

WHAT ARE REPORTERS' RIGHTS?

Some reporters express concern that if their "hunch" is mistaken they may be civilly sued for slander. However, most state statutes provide immunity from civil or criminal liability. For example,

> Any person who makes a report . . . shall be immune from any civil
> or criminal liability . . . unless such person acted in bad faith or with
> a malicious purpose. (Va. Code Ann., 2017b)

Mandatory reporters are also permitted to release information that is otherwise confidential without penalty.

IS THERE A PENALTY FOR NOT REPORTING?

States may impose a civil penalty or criminal (most frequently a misdemeanor) sanctions on mandated reporters who fail to make a required report.[1] In Virginia, for example, the civil statute reads:

> Any person who fails to make a required report or notification pursuant to subsection A shall be subject to a civil penalty of not more than $500 for the first failure and not less than $100 nor more than $1,000 for any subsequent failures. (Va. Code Ann., 2017c)

However, in practice mandatory reporting laws typically are not enforced (Kohn, 2003).

WHAT WILL HAPPEN NEXT?

Chapter 5 provides detailed information on the operation of APS. For the purposes of this chapter, however, APS will receive the report and evaluate it to determine whether it meets certain eligibility criteria. If it does, the case will be assigned to an APS caseworker for investigation, which in most states requires a face-to-face interview with the victim within some statutorily determined number of days. On completion of the investigation, the APS caseworker will make a disposition (i.e., a decision as to whether there was more credible evidence than not that the reported abuse occurred). Depending on the disposition, the APS caseworker

---

[1] See http://www.americanbar.org/content/dam/aba/administrative/law_aging/2011/2011_aging_ea_ failure.authcheckdam.pdf for a comparison chart of penalties for each U.S. state, territory, and the District of Columbia.

may arrange for or provide services to the client. However, the clinician (reporter) may or may not be informed of any or all of these activities.

Notification to Reporters

It is sometimes asserted that APS does not respond to reports of abuse, dampening a reporter's enthusiasm for reporting (Balaswamy, 2004). There are several possible explanations for this perception. APS must comply with strict eligibility criteria before opening a case (Wolf, 2001), and if the facts do not meet the criteria, then the case will not be opened for an investigation (i.e., the case is invalid). If a case meets eligibility criteria and is opened, confidentiality restrictions may prohibit APS caseworkers from contacting the reporter to inform them that an investigation was completed (although this, too, varies by state). The perception of nonresponsiveness may be further facilitated by the mobility of APS caseworkers who spend a considerable proportion of their work time in the field visiting clients in their homes, making actual contact with caseworkers challenging (Balaswamy, 2004). If an investigation was undertaken but the finding was inconclusive or unfounded, the case would be closed, making it appear as though nothing happened. Furthermore, based on the principle of self-determination, competent elder abuse victims in all states can refuse services (U.S. Government Accountability Office, 2011), which again may appear to the reporter that no action was taken by APS. Given these various circumstances, it is clear that reporters rarely learn from the APS caseworker the status or result of the investigation (although this varies by state) and therefore sometimes assume that their reporting was for naught (Balaswamy, 2004).

Reporters want to be kept in the loop because they want to know that their reporting made a difference (Feng, Fetzer, Chen, Yeh, & Huang, 2010). It is important that some state statutes do permit closing this feedback loop by contacting the reporter after a determination has been made (e.g., Annotated Laws of Massachusetts, 2016). However, most states are silent on this issue, in which case confidentiality may trump closing the feedback loop. Clinicians wishing to be notified are encouraged to explicitly request that the APS caseworker notify the clinician at the close of the investigation (although a response cannot be guaranteed).

CONCLUSION

Detection of elder abuse remains problematic in the United States. Detection is hampered by whether and how abuse is perceived, and victims and professionals often perceive an abusive situation differently. Understanding how older victims perceive—or fail to perceive—abuse may assist clinicians in raising awareness among their older clients. However, once detected, there remains understandable reluctance among older adults and those around them to report elder abuse. Understanding the reasons for this reluctance will facilitate clinicians' conversations with older adults about their own reporting obligations. Therefore, in addition to the general reporting principles outlined in this chapter, clinicians will need to learn their state's requirements and rights. Contact the state's board of psychology for state-specific information on elder abuse mandatory reporting.

5

Working With the Adult Protective Services System

The extent to which clinicians have occasion to interface with adult protective services (APS) can vary. Circumstances under which clinicians may encounter APS might include whether the clinician needs to place a report with APS over concerns about mistreatment and whether their client is either experiencing abuse or mistreating an older adult. Conversely, clinicians may interface with APS when APS makes a client referral to a clinician for either an assessment (e.g., capacity assessment, neuropsychological evaluation) or treatment or counseling. As recommended by the American Psychological Association (APA; 2014) "Guidelines for Psychological Practice With Older Adults," clinicians working with older adults should collaborate with APS (p. 54). Therefore, it is important to understand how APS and the service providers within that system operate.

http://dx.doi.org/10.1037/0000056-005
Understanding Elder Abuse: A Clinician's Guide, by S. L. Jackson

THE APS CASEWORKER'S PROFILE

Jogerst, Daly, and Ingram (2003) conducted the only national survey of APS caseworkers. They found that APS caseworkers are on average 46.4 years of age (range = 22–75 years), 76% are female, 49% hold a college degree, and they have worked on average 9 years in their current position (range = 1 month–35 years). Sommerfeld, Henderson, Snider, and Aarons (2014) reported caseloads of between 30 and 35 clients. Anecdotally, it is often asserted that low pay and high turnover plague this profession. Professionals in this field often lack adequate training and cross-training (Brandl, 2011; Connell-Carrick & Scannapieco, 2008). Testifying before the U.S. Senate Special Committee on Aging (2011), on observing that not all states require training for APS caseworkers, Quinn (2013) incredulously stated that "Starbucks employees have to go through 40 hours of training, but not an APS caseworker who is making 'life-and-death decisions' about elder abuse victims" (p. 23). It is unclear whether there is a sufficient troop of caseworkers to respond to the needs of minority victims (Connell-Carrick & Scannapieco, 2008).

THE OPERATION OF APS

APS are situated in civil, not criminal, law. Every state has a civil system for reporting and responding to elder abuse (Bonnie & Wallace, 2003; U.S. Government Accountability Office [GAO], 2011), typically referred to as APS.[1] That is, APS is statutorily charged with receiving reports of abuse, investigating allegations, making a disposition, and assisting victims in remedying the situation by providing or arranging services for those deemed in need of protective services (see Figure 5.1). Although statutes (and administrative policy) typically guide the actions of APS caseworkers, they do not necessarily dictate their ideology (Jackson & Hafemeister, 2013a).

---

[1] In most states, elder abuse occurring in long-term care facilities (e.g., nursing homes) is handled by local long-term care (LTC) ombudsmen. LTC ombudsmen programs accept reports of elder abuse occurring in nursing homes, assisted living facilities, and board and care homes. LTC ombudsmen are advocates for residents; they do not engage in investigations on behalf of the state, which is the exclusive jurisdiction of state APS and/or law enforcement, depending on the state. In only about half the states does APS have jurisdiction in LTC facilities.

Aspects of elder abuse (i.e., the definition, mandated r
investigation, capacity issues, and the responses available t
workers), governed by state statute and administrative polic
differ by state (Jirik & Sanders, 2014). As reviewed in Chap
vary in how they define a victim of elder abuse. Their crit
based on (a) victim age (e.g., 65 years of age), (b) victim vul
(c) victim age and vulnerability, or (d) no restriction on the v
anyone could be a victim—the state has no restriction or eligib
ria). Only six states have criteria for defining offenders of elder a
caretaker/trusted other). It should be noted that not only do AP
vary between states but also within states, with many APS agen
county—rather than state—administered. Therefore, rates of su
tion vary between counties and jurisdictions even within the sa
(Mosqueda et al., 2016).

It is estimated that one in 24 cases of elder abuse is reporte
authorities (Lachs & Berman, 2011), suggesting that APS is inves
relatively few of the elder abuse cases actually occurring in the comr
However, once a report is received, if the allegation meets certair
bility criteria (also defined in statute and administrative policy), th
is assigned to an APS caseworker for investigation. Because states
elder abuse differently, each state has adopted their own screening p
dures (or eligibility criteria), which means that at least some victims
might access services in one state would not be eligible to access servic
another. Typically, state statute stipulates the amount of time within w
contact with the victim must be made (typically not more than 72 h
depending on the situation). The investigation likely involves visiting
victim in their own home to conduct a face-to-face interview (but it ma
conducted by telephone under certain circumstances). The investigat
is a proactive undertaking on the part of APS and is perceived by some
intrusive and even potentially dangerous for victims. For example, hor
visits, collateral interviews, leaving literature, and contact with or notific
tion of the abusive individual may place some older victims in jeopar

---

[2]This book focuses on older adults. However, many states' APS agencies also serve adults wit
disabilities.

epo
o AP,
, frequ
ter 4, states
ria may be
nerability,[2]
victim (i.e.,
ility crite-
abuse (i.e.,
agencies
ies being
bstantia-
me state

d to the
igating
munity.
eligi-
e case
define
roce-
who
es in
hich
ours
the
be
on
as
e
a-
y

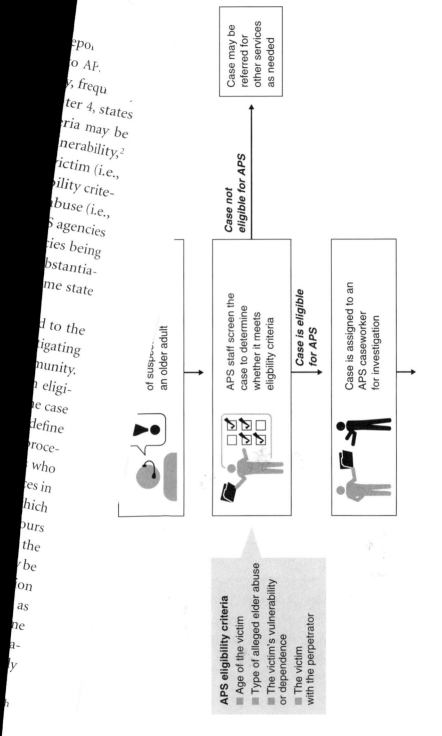

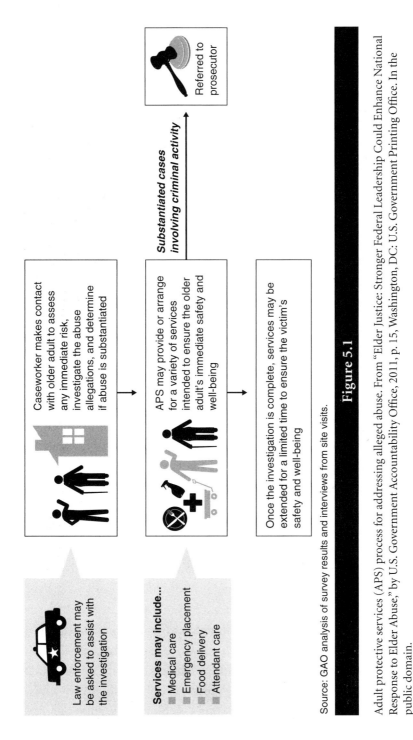

Law enforcement may be asked to assist with the investigation

Caseworker makes contact with older adult to assess any immediate risk, investigate the abuse allegations, and determine if abuse is substantiated

Services may include...
- Medical care
- Emergency placement
- Food delivery
- Attendant care

APS may provide or arrange for a variety of services intended to ensure the older adult's immediate safety and well-being

Once the investigation is complete, services may be extended for a limited time to ensure the victim's safety and well-being

Substantiated cases involving criminal activity

Referred to prosecutor

Source: GAO analysis of survey results and interviews from site visits.

Figure 5.1

Adult protective services (APS) process for addressing alleged abuse. From "Elder Justice: Stronger Federal Leadership Could Enhance National Response to Elder Abuse," by U.S. Government Accountability Office, 2011, p. 15, Washington, DC: U.S. Government Printing Office. In the public domain.

by alerting the abusive individual to the APS investigation, for example, in abuse in later life cases (Brandl, 2011). It is important to note that the purpose of an APS investigation is not to determine whether a crime has been committed (Dyer, Heisler, Hill, & Kim, 2005), but rather whether a person is in need of protective services (eligibility), and if they are in need, to offer or arrange (not compel) services.

If warranted, APS caseworkers in every state conduct some type of capacity screen of their clients because capacity is foundational to the remainder of the investigation (Falk & Hoffman, 2014). That is, if a victim has capacity, they have the right to refuse an investigation in most states and to refuse services in all states (GAO, 2011; Jackson, 2017a).

Historically, there has been relatively little interaction or collaboration between APS and law enforcement. However, state statutes frequently have a provision stipulating when APS must contact law enforcement (e.g., if a crime is suspected to have occurred). There may be many reasons why APS caseworkers do not refer instances of elder abuse to law enforcement, but they have received little systematic inquiry.

Although there are exceptions (Payne, Berg, & Toussaint, 2001), law enforcement personnel routinely fail to refer elder abuse cases to APS, although they are mandated reporters in most states. This failure may be in part because they are unaware of the services APS can provide or because they believe they can or have resolved the matter satisfactorily (Daniels, Baumhover, Formby, & Clark-Daniels, 1999). Furthermore, law enforcement has been reluctant to directly respond to allegations of elder abuse. For example, Brownell (2005) contended that most law enforcement officers do not consider financial exploitation a criminal matter. Relatedly, they may be less adept at responding to cases involving family members (Payne & Berg, 2003), and, unfortunately, many elder abuse cases involve complex and intransigent family dynamics (Band-Winterstein, Avieli, & Smeloy, 2016). However, when law enforcement and APS fail to collaborate, there can be "lost or degraded critical evidence or witnesses" (Heisler & Stiegel, 2004, p. 41), a failure to hold offenders accountable or deter future offenses, or a lost opportunity to recognize and respond appropriately to the needs and wishes of the victim. Unequivocally, apprehending

and punishing the abusive individual is the exclusive resp
enforcement (Payne, 2011), whereas APS focuses on th
& Zielke, 2005). However, greater collaboration can res
comes for the victim as well as the criminal justice system (Gassoumis,
Navarro, & Wilber, 2015; Navarro, Gassoumis, & Wilber, 2013).

Once an APS investigation has been completed, there are typically four
potential dispositions (i.e., a decision as to whether there was more credible evidence than not that the reported abuse occurred): (a) the client
is in need of services and accepts, (b) the client is in need of services and
declines, (c) the need for protective services no longer exists (e.g., the abusive individual no longer has access to the client), or (d) the case is un-
substantiated (i.e., unfounded or insufficient evidence). The disposition
is typically based on the judgment of the individual APS caseworker using
the *preponderance of the evidence* standard (Mosqueda & Olsen, 2015).
To be designated a "victim" and eligible for protective services under
this regime requires a disposition of "in need of protective services and
accepts." Otherwise, the case likely will be closed.

The practice of APS is guided by the principle of *self-determination*
(Bergeron, 2000, 2006; National Adult Protective Services Association,
2015). Self-determination is a person's ability to think, choose, decide,
and act on his or her own free from coercion (Ekelund, Dahlin-Ivanoff, &
Eklund, 2014). Related to the principle of self-determination is the principle of *autonomy*; both are terms that are sometimes used interchange-
ably but have an important distinction (Ekelund et al., 2014). Autonomy
comprises three principles, one of which is self-determination; that is,
(a) self-determination or personal agency, (b) independence or freedom
from coercion when making a decision (i.e., free will), and (c) rationality
or the ability to reflect critically on one's desires and beliefs (Miller, 1995).
A good decision, then, is one that satisfies an individual's desires, prefer-
ences, and expectations, no matter whether they are in conformity with
societal values (Fan, 1997, p. 315).

The Western conceptualization of autonomy, in which the older
adult has the final say in a decision, may operate differently between gen-
ders (O'Connor, Hall, & Donnelly, 2009) and is distinguishable from the

conceptualization of autonomy in other cultures (Fan, 1997). In Asian cultures, for example, family determination, rather than self-determination, is the organizing principle (Fan, 1997). If a family member becomes sick, it is the responsibility of the entire family to care for her or him. Therefore, decisions are made by arriving at an agreement through cooperation with other relevant persons rather than the older adult making a decision based solely on her or his own desire.

REFUSAL OF INVESTIGATION AND/OR SERVICES

For elder abuse victims with *capacity* (i.e., the ability to reason, remember complex information, set goals, oriented to time and place, and self-identify), the principle of self-determination is reflected in the practice of honoring their right to refuse services and is articulated as such in each state's statute (GAO, 2011). Studies generally find that up to a quarter of APS clients decline services (Clancy, McDaid, O'Neill, & O'Brien, 2011), with one study finding that victims of physical abuse were significantly more likely to refuse services than were victims of three other forms of abuse (Jackson & Hafemeister, 2012a).

Older victims may have legitimate explanations for refusing services. They are similar to the reasons older victims choose not to self-report and include the following:

- fear of being institutionalized (Jackson & Hafemeister, 2014; Wright, 2010),
- being (financially or physically) dependent on the abuser,
- not wanting to get their loved one in trouble (Beaulaurier, Seff, Newman, & Dunlop, 2005),
- loyalty (love) to and protection of relatives and caregivers (Jackson & Hafemeister, 2015), and
- a belief that services will make the situation worse than the problem (DeMichele, Crowe, & Stigel, 2007).

Refusal of services is often interpreted as a defect in the older adult's decision making. Ironically, this may trigger a cognitive assessment, which may ultimately result in the imposition of a court-ordered intervention. However, it may be that older victims assess the situation through a different lens than professionals, taking into consideration factors other than their own safety (Bergeron, 2006; O'Connor et al., 2009; Wright, 2010), particularly if the abusive individual is a family member (Band-Winterstein et al., 2016; Jackson & Hafemeister, 2016). The victim's preferred courses of action may be shaped by broader considerations, such as concern for the family member's well-being, a desire to maintain a relationship with this person, various social norms regarding familial obligations, and a need for emotional and instrumental assistance from the abusive individual (Aschbrenner, Greenberg, Allen, & Seltzer, 2010). Furthermore, victims may not even perceive their safety as being in jeopardy to the extent that an APS caseworker might (Jackson & Hafemeister, 2013a). Further complicating the situation is that autonomy may be impaired by depression, threats, or other influences, and it may not be clear whether their choice to refuse services is based on true volition (Bergeron, 2006; O'Connor et al., 2009).

Clearly, more could be done in the name of compassionate interference to win a client's confidence through persuasion (Jackson & Hafemeister, 2013a; Regan, 1981) rather than adhering to the false dichotomy of coercion or inaction (Verkerk, 1999). Professionals who come into contact with older adults who refuse services are advised to recognize the inherent power differential between the helper and the helpee (O'Connor et al., 2009; Verkerk, 1999) and to engage the client rather than immediately accept their refusal. As clinicians know, engagement is a process rather than an event and clearly takes more time than most APS caseworkers are allotted (Bergeron, 2006; Jackson & Hafemeister, 2013a), which is typically 45 days from investigation to disposition. Repeated attempts to build rapport with the victim might be necessary, while identifying and recognizing the fears experienced by older victims and offering services for their abuser. Clinicians are advised to adhere to these same recommendations in the context of working with older clients.

APS has been denigrated because not all cases of elder abuse are resolved (Burnes, Rizzo, & Courtney, 2014; Comijs, Pot, Smit, Bouter, & Jonker, 1998;

Jackson & Hafemeister, 2013b; Sommerfeld, Henderson, Snider, & Aarons, 2014), which may be in part because of the victim's right to refuse services. In fact, clients who refuse services have an 11.9% increase in having a subsequent report to APS (National Council on Crime and Delinquency, 2013). The easy cases are those in which an older adult clearly has capacity or clearly lacks capacity. The significant challenge for APS caseworkers lies in the gray area between these two conditions, with APS at times having to lay wait until an older adult's capacity diminishes to the point where intervention can be imposed. Refusal of services may be the greatest obstacle to successful intervention, with many of these cases becoming "revolving door" cases (Sommerfeld et al., 2014).

PROVISION OR ARRANGEMENT OF SERVICES

Given the differences in exposure and victim characteristics (Emery & Laumann-Billings, 1998), there may be some victims who are able to respond to their needs on their own, while others need varying degrees of assistance. Studies indicate that victim needs fall along a continuum from none (Newmark, 2006) to numerous (Macy, Giattina, Sangster, Crosby, & Montijo, 2009), although this has not been as well documented in the elder abuse context. However, Alon and Berg-Warman (2014) found that the higher the number of services implemented, the lower the rate of improvement. The authors opined that this may be because cases involving individuals with multiple needs are more complex and difficult to "fix." Furthermore, it has been suggested that victims may have a range of service needs that vary by the type of abuse experienced (Lachs & Pillemer, 2015; Moye & Braun, 2010; Nerenberg, 2008; Payne, 2011; Penhale, 2010). However, the number and type of service needs by type of elder abuse, or by victim–offender relationship, has not been well assessed.

APS are designed to provide assistance and protection to victims. Service provision is stipulated in state statutes, although it varies by state (Jackson, 2017a). In all but four states the statutory language specifies that APS may "provide *or* arrange" for services. All but 10 state statutes list permissible voluntary services, typically worded as "services including

Table 5.1

Services Identified in at Least Two State Statutes

Service category	Examples of services
Civil and criminal legal	Protective–restraining orders, restitution, law-enforcement referral, court accompaniment, eviction notices
Medical	Medical evaluation, medical supplies, home health aid
Out-of-home residence	Relocation, voluntary institutional placement, assistance in locating a domestic violence shelter
In-home residential assistance	In-home services, chores–homemaker services, adequate heat and ventilation
Mental health services	Counseling, psychiatric, support groups, skills training to address ambivalence
Financial management	Assistance with financial debt–creditors, applying for a representative payee, applying for public benefits, emergency financial assistance
Personal needs	Transportation, food, clothing, hygiene, adult day care
Case management	Coordinate services
Guardianship services	Locate a public or private guardian; arrange for a guardianship hearing

but not limited to. . . ." Table 5.1 lists services identified in at least two state statutes. Although clinicians will not be involved in providing the majority of the services listed in Table 5.1, an older adult may be referred by APS to a clinician for mental health services. Clinicians may be involved in short-term counseling services, referring a client to a psychiatrist for cases involving a serious mental illness, facilitating support groups, or skills training to address ambivalence on the part of older parent–adult child relationships (see, e.g., Luescher & Pillemer, 1998). Currently, there are no mental health protocols to address elder abuse. Clinicians are nonetheless urged to use their clinical skills in identifying and treating the clinical needs of older victims while adhering to the APA (2014) recommendations for working with older adults. Recently, Burnes and Lachs (2017) have advocated for developing and monitoring clients' goals through the use of goal-attainment scaling.

In the context of elder abuse, clinicians must be cognizant that mental health services are but one of many services older adults may be receiving. Clinicians should be aware of the other services available to victims of elder abuse to help form their recommendations. For example, clinicians may be involved in the diagnosis of diminished financial capacity. Services that could be recommended with such a diagnosis include money management, utility company third-party notification, shared bank account, durable or springing power of attorney, and representative payee programs (Moye & Braun, 2010).

To familiarize clinicians with the banquet of services to which older victims may have access, three studies that have documented the services actually provided to victims of elder abuse through APS are reviewed. Clancy et al. (2011) reported that of the 2,391 client interventions, monitoring (21%) was predominant, along with home support (19%) and counseling or support (18%); followed by long-term care (11%), respite care (11%), and referrals for other services (11%). Less frequently used were adult day care (4%), advocacy (4%), and mediation or conflict resolution (2%). Lithwick, Beaulieu, Gravel, and Straka (1999) found that interventions for cases involving abusers who were adult offspring included homemaker services (46%), private services (41%), external medical services (39%), in-house medical services (36%), placement of the victim (30%), legal services (28%), residence or group home placements (21%), psychiatric intervention (10%), and interim placement (8%). Choi, Kulick, and Mayer (1999) reviewed financial exploitation cases and found services specific to these victims included case management (67%), financial management–representative or protective payee (64%), establishment of guardianship (13%), establishment of power of attorney (4%), petition for conservatorship (2%), legal–court sanction or order of protection against the abusive individual (9.1%), admission to a residential facility (4%), and continued monitoring of suspected abuse–neglect (14%). Restraining orders, prominent in the intimate partner violence arena (Sorenson & Shen, 2005), appear to be an underused intervention in the context of elder abuse (Choi et al., 1999). Curiously, no state has enacted a provision to remedy or alleviate social isolation, thought by some to be a relatively robust risk

factor for elder abuse (e.g., Acierno et al., 2010), or ⸜
for offenders.

UNDERSTANDING INVOLUNTARY INTERVEN

Clinicians must understand that a report to APS may on occasion result in APS taking a more interventionist role than the caseworker might like, that is, when the victim lacks capacity or is in immediate danger (Bonnie & Wallace, 2003, p. 126). Under carefully proscribed circumstances, involuntary interventions by APS are legally authorized. For example, persons deemed to be incompetent may not have the ability to protect themselves, in which case the state has a duty to intervene on their behalf (Falk & Hoffman, 2014). As mentioned, APS intervenes on behalf of the state under the doctrine of *parens patriae*, or the state may act as a parent, a principle grounded in beneficence (Falk & Hoffman, 2014; Winick, 1995). This type of intervention is justified by the view that the harm caused by limiting an individual's autonomy is exceeded by the benefit of ensuring the incompetent person's receipt of services. The two primary legal mechanisms for imposing services on an incompetent person are civil commitment and guardianship (Regan, 1981), each of which requires prior judicial authorization. Such interventions have the potential to severely limit a person's freedom of choice and as a result trigger due process safeguards (Regan, 1981; Winick, 1995). A judicial finding of incompetency is, thus, a prerequisite for APS acting as a government agent to take actions that promote the best interests of the incompetent older adult. APS cannot impose such actions unilaterally but must first obtain a court order with the procedural safeguards accompanying it. Although originally conceptualized as pertaining only to mental incapacity, physical incapacity has been subsumed under the rubric of incapacity in the context of elder abuse (Regan, 1981).

APS caseworkers have developed a reputation for imposing involuntary interventions, such as removing older adults involuntarily from their homes (for safety purposes) or placing them under guardianship, a practice believed to curb the appetite of some professionals to report. However, in reality, less than 10% of substantiated elder abuse cases involve involuntary actions (Duke, 1997). Across several studies, approximately 10% of elder abuse victims are institutionalized following contact with APS (Clancy et al., 2011; Thomson et al., 2011), although it is unclear whether institutionalization was voluntary or involuntary. Dyer et al. (2005) concluded that fewer than 7% of cases result in legal interventions, such as guardianship. Linda Farber Post (as cited in Naik, Lai, Kunik, & Dyer, 2008) reminded us that honoring the wishes of a person with capacity demonstrates respect for the individual, but honoring the wishes of a person without capacity is a form of abandonment. Clinicians must recognize that there are times when APS must intervene against the wishes of an older adult; however, to reiterate, APS does not have the power to impose involuntary interventions on their own but only through a court order.

OUTCOMES OF AND SATISFACTION WITH SERVICES PROVIDED BY APS

APS has often been criticized for engaging in practices that are not evidence based, primarily because very little research has explored their practices (Moore & Browne, 2016; Pillemer, Connolly, Breckman, Spreng, & Lachs, 2015). There is evidence that even a report of abuse to APS (let alone the investigation) increases the likelihood of institutionalization (Dong & Simon, 2013a) as well as mortality (Dong et al., 2009). However, when APS caseworkers are asked, they tend to perceive their interventions (e.g., institutionalization) as effective (Dolon & Blakely, 1989).

The outcomes associated with an APS investigation, such as a change in living arrangement, separation from the offender, and guardianship, may result in safety for older adults, but older victims have not been asked about their satisfaction with those (voluntary or involuntary) outcomes. As reviewed earlier, APS caseworkers and older adults sometimes hold different views of the underlying causes of abuse (Jackson & Hafemeister, 2013a), suggesting they might perceive outcomes differently as well. Further complicating the situation is a study finding that the service most frequently offered (i.e., social services) was not the type of service that had the greatest impact (i.e., legal services) on the abusive situation (Alon &

Berg-Warman, 2014). The field has yet to identify and define su
outcomes (either voluntary or involuntary) much beyond the c
of abuse (Burnes et al., 2014).

REALISTIC EXPECTATIONS OF APS

It is sometimes expected (or at least desired) that APS can intervene in a
situation and resolve all existing problems. It is the case that the more severe
the problem becomes, the more the power shifts from the family to the system (i.e., APS; Eisikovits, Koren, & Band-Winterstein, 2013, p. 5). And yet,
as noted earlier, not all cases of elder abuse are resolved (Burnes et al., 2014;
Jackson & Hafemeister, 2013b; Sommerfeld et al., 2014). APS responds to
the neediest of victims with limited resources (Jackson, 2017a). Although
a continuum of complexity exists (Jackson & Hafemeister, 2015), many
cases are complex, reflecting years of interpersonal dysfunction. In some
cases, these situations only come to the attention of authorities such as
APS later in life. Juxtapose this reality of elder abuse against the reality and
intention that by statute, APS interventions are typically short-term and
relatively superficial (Jackson, 2017a). Once the investigation is completed,
APS often enlists community organizations to provide longer term comprehensive services (Quinn & Benson, 2012; Wolf, 2001). However, even
those services may be insufficient to effect the kind of change needed. The
mismatch of need versus service may contribute to perceptions that the
field is producing less-than-optimal outcomes for victims. Mental health
services may be an exception (depending on the community). Clinicians
may have the latitude to effect greater change in situations that allow for
the provision of longer term mental health services.

RESPONDING THROUGH
MULTIDISCIPLINARY TEAMS

One practice that is growing in prominence is responding to elder abuse
cases through multidisciplinary teams (Anetzberger, 2011; Breckman,
Callahan, & Solomon, 2015; Pillemer et al., 2015). Elder abuse, including financial exploitation, cases are frequently complex, as they involve

navigating family conflict and complex financial instruments. Therefore, these cases necessitate greater time as well as resources (Swanson & Brownell, 2013). Because of this complexity, communities are turning to elder abuse multidisciplinary teams. The two key assumptions associated with multidisciplinary teams are that complex cases require a complex response and no one system can address all the needs—physical, psychological, emotional, intellectual, familial, interpersonal, financial, social, cultural, and spiritual— of an older victim (Dyer et al., 2005). Services must be tailored to the needs of the individual, necessitating the availability of a smorgasbord of services and interventions at any given time—a goal that is more easily accomplished through coordination and collaboration among service providers.

Multidisciplinary teams also promote the inclusion of professionals who have historically been absent from society's formal response to elder abuse, in this case, mental health professionals. Psychologists and other mental health clinicians are encouraged to participate on elder abuse multidisciplinary teams (APA, 2014; Scheiderer, 2012; Wiglesworth, Kemp, & Mosqueda, 2008). Clinical psychologists, neuropsychologists, geriatric psychiatrists, and other mental health clinicians can provide information to a criminal investigator looking to establish the vulnerability of an alleged victim, or a prosecutor assessing the ability of an alleged victim to serve as a witness to his or her own abuse (Mosqueda & Olsen, 2015; Scheiderer, 2012; Wiglesworth et al., 2008). Furthermore, they can provide information on the conditions associated with abuse, available mental health interventions, insight into family dynamics, and how best to respond to a victim's particular goals and values while not violating confidentiality (Karel, 2011). For example, consider this case:

> At the case review meeting, the multidisciplinary team coordinator recapped the case of 78-year-old Mrs. Z involving physical abuse by her husband, ending with "Well, team, what's the plan? Are there services we're missing?" This situation is long-term and high risk. Mrs. Z lives in senior subsidized housing with her husband, but her three sons live with them and sleep on the floor. Mrs. Z will lose her housing if the Housing Authority learns her sons live there. The multidisciplinary team members queried whether

Mrs. Z's sons were protective in that her husband does not beat her when the boys are there, or whether the boys are also abusing her. The APS caseworker was unable to confirm either way. The team agreed not to address the sons living in the home until their role could be determined. The team discussed Mrs. Z's weight, suggesting she either has an eating disorder or fails to eat when she feels anxious, as she is now 87 pounds. The multidisciplinary team coordinator suggested making sure she at least has Ensure to keep her alive. A community-based mental health provider on the team visits Mrs. Z weekly under the guise of a community advocate and agreed to supply Mrs. Z with Ensure while "checking" on her. Mrs. Z's case was put on the next month's meeting agenda at which time the team will reassess the situation.

A multidisciplinary team offers improved evidence-gathering techniques and support for victims. However, only nine states have an elder abuse multidisciplinary team statute (excluding elder fatality review teams; Daly & Jogerst, 2014), suggesting that this approach has not gained traction among legislators. The practice, however, is growing nationally. The empirical validation of multidisciplinary teams is quite small. Navarro et al. (2013) found that financial exploitation cases funneled through a multidisciplinary team were more likely to be referred to the prosecutor, and victims were more likely to have a conservator appointed (Gassoumis et al., 2015). Alon and Berg-Warman (2014) found that working within a multidisciplinary team increased the morale of APS caseworkers and increased the likelihood of interventions for abusive individuals.

CONCLUSION

Clinicians involved with an elder abuse case will be interfacing with APS in one way or another. To work more effectively, and to manage expectations, it is important for clinicians to understand how APS operates, the limitations within which they work, and the services they provide. The reality is that the practice of APS continues to be based on experience rather than empirical evidence (Pillemer et al., 2015), and the effectiveness of an APS investigation and service provision is largely unknown.

Arguably, the current system of response—APS—treats the symptoms of elder abuse through the provision of short-term superficial services but not the underlying causes (Dunlop, Rothman, Condon, Hebert, & Martinez, 2001). APS caseworkers have the unenviable task of continually navigating between the principles of self-determination and paternalism (Burnes, 2016). The reality is that in some cases, adherence to the principle of self-determination will result in elder abuse persisting unchecked (Glick, 2005), as older adults with capacity have the right to refuse services in all states. Involuntary interventions can only be imposed under strict circumstances and only with a court order. Society's expectations of APS may be too high given their limited resources and scope. Nonetheless, more can be done to assist older victims. One action clinicians can take to move the needle is to join a multidisciplinary team to benefit victims as well as other professionals serving on the team.

6

Elder Abuse Interventions

As reviewed in Chapter 4, efforts are underway to increase the reporting of elder abuse, under the belief that funneling victims into the system will enable their receipt of services and interventions. As recommended by the American Psychological Association (APA) "Guidelines for Psychological Practice With Older Adults" (2014, pp. 37–38), this chapter is designed to familiarize clinicians with elder abuse interventions, many of which are relatively new. Clinicians will quickly observe that mental health interventions are essentially absent from the cache of interventions. To provide some context for this section, a brief history of elder abuse interventions is provided.

PERSPECTIVE ON SERVICES AND INTERVENTIONS

Historically, there have been two primary ways of responding in elder abuse cases: (a) maintaining victim–offender relationship through providing caregiver supports (e.g., respite care); and (b) separating

http://dx.doi.org/10.1037/0000056-006
Understanding Elder Abuse: A Clinician's Guide, by S. L. Jackson

, from their offenders to obtain safety, through a change in liv-
.rrangement, imposition of guardianship, or through offender
ρ. secution.

Respite Care to Maintain Victim–Offender Relationship

Family care remains the most prevalent method of eldercare, even for
those with severe disabilities such as Alzheimer's disease (Doty, 2010;
see Larson & Kao, 2016, for a review). The caregiver stress model so
pervasive in the 1970s spurred the respite care industry as an intervention for elder abuse. This intervention remains prominent today
(Ayalon, Lev, Green, & Nevo, 2016; Lindland, Fond, Haydon, & Kendall-
Taylor, 2015), even while support for the caregiver stress model is waning
(Jackson & Hafemeister, 2013d).

Separation of Victim and Offender

The other primary intervention has been to separate the victim from the
offender through various means. For example, one intervention designed
to safeguard incapacitated older adults is guardianship. However, safety
may be achieved for older adults with capacity by placement in a long-
term care facility. Although some modifications in living arrangements
are the result of safety concerns for older victims, an implicit underlying purpose of changing the victim's living arrangement is to separate
the older victim from the offender, especially when the two have been
cohabitating, a particularly common living situation among older victims of interpersonal violence (O'Keeffe et al., 2007). Not unsurprisingly,
Alon and Berg-Warman (2014) found that separating the older victim
from the offender resulted in a reduction in violence. However, separation
is not typically the desire of the older victim, especially in cases involving
family members (Harbison, Coughlan, Karabanow, & VanderPlaat, 2005;
Mariam, McClure, Robinson, & Yang, 2015).

Another approach designed in part to separate victims from their
abusers is prosecution. Prosecution has been the primary intervention

in elder abuse cases, although prosecution rates are astonishingly low (Meirson, 2008), and prosecution may not be the most effective intervention (Jackson, 2016a). Separation through prosecution may provide but a temporary respite for the older person, as at some point the abusive individual will be released and may return to the older person's home, presenting a renewed risk of abuse (Jackson & Hafemeister, 2014). Furthermore, relatively few older adults are interested in pursuing prosecution (Jackson & Hafemeister, 2013c). This stance has spurred the development of victimless prosecution. However, Kohn (2012) admonished clinicians to listen to voices of victims in this matter.

CURRENT STATE OF ELDER ABUSE INTERVENTIONS

The field of elder abuse has placed very little effort into intervention development (Du Mont, Kosa, Macdonald, Elliot, & Yaffe, 2015; Pillemer, Connolly, Breckman, Spreng, & Lachs, 2015). Several reviews of elder abuse interventions have been published (e.g., Moore & Browne, 2016; O'Donnell, Phelan, & Fealy, 2015). Ayalon et al. (2016) recently reviewed the elder abuse intervention literature and found only 24 studies, 19 of which concerned caregiver interventions. Another review of the literature concluded that interventions currently being used to protect and assist the victims of elder abuse are relatively ineffective and sometimes even counterproductive (Moore & Browne, 2016). For example, Davis and Medina-Ariza (2001) field tested an elder abuse intervention program in New York City based on a successful domestic violence intervention. One of the findings was that households that received home visits (both in project and nonproject dwellings) called the police more often than control households. However, by 12 months the effect had disappeared. The researchers speculate that elder abuse victims are often dependent on their abusers in multiple ways and, compared with domestic violence victims, may have even less hope of gaining independence from their abusers. This study was exceptional given that many interventions fail to even evaluate their effectiveness, let alone unintended negative effects (Pillemer, Mueller-Johnson, Mock, Suitor, & Lachs, 2007).

ABUSE PROGRAMS AND INTERVENTIONS TARGETING VICTIMS

multitude of small programs across the country designed to a̲ ̲ ̲ ̲er abuse. None are large in scale, and few have been evaluated to any extent. However, several programs warrant review here.

Victim Services Programs

The need for victim services in the context of elder abuse has been publicly proclaimed (U.S. Senate Special Committee on Aging, 2015). Elder Care, Inc., in Louisville, Kentucky, is an elder abuse victim service program responding to the needs of victims of all forms of elder abuse. All police reports where the victim is over the age of 60 are automatically electronically relayed to Elder Care. The victim advocate reaches out to the victim to provide traditional victim services (e.g., court accompaniment, accessing victim compensation, orders of protection, victim impact statements). One unique way in which Elder Care responds to the needs of older adults is by driving or transporting them to court to get an emergency protective order and any follow-up hearings. However, if the older adult is physically unable to go to court for a protective order, a hearing over the phone can be arranged. One advocate stays with the victim in their home while another advocate is in the courtroom. Elder Care also employs a social worker who ensures the older victim is linked with needed services in the community. The program, however, has yet to be evaluated.

Elder Abuse Shelters

The use of domestic violence shelters for older victims has been problematic in that they fail to meet the unique needs of older adults (Fisher, Zink, Pabst, Regan, & Rinto, 2003). For example, medically and/or psychiatrically dependent older adults are not able to function without assistance, a service not offered by most shelters. However, The Harry & Jeanette Weinberg Center for Elder Abuse Prevention developed wraparound services for older victims that includes shelter within an established long-term care facility, a model that is being replicated in other communities (Solomon & Reingold, 2012) but has yet to be evaluated.

Civil Legal Assistance Program

A notable shortcoming in our response to elder abuse has been the lack of civil legal assistance to older adults. Pennsylvania, however, through its Senior Law Center, provides civil legal assistance to older adults. The National Association of Senior Legal Hotlines, of which Pennsylvania is a member, provides assistance to seniors over the phone initially, and then where appropriate, refers the older adult to assistance in their local area. Maine Legal Services for the Elderly likewise provides civil legal assistance to victims of elder abuse and is working tirelessly to remedy financial exploitation cases. Los Angeles also has a notable program, Bet Tzedek Legal Services, which provides free legal services to seniors and employs a social worker to do a quick assessment of older callers and make referrals if warranted (Morris, 2010).

Hospital-Based Elder Abuse Examiner Program

Building on the success of Sexual Assault Nurse Examiner (SANE) programs across the county, Canada has developed a program in which SANEs are being trained to become Elder Abuse Nurse Examiners (EANEs) in hospitals. A curriculum is being developed to ensure EANEs are able to recognize elder abuse, understand the dynamics of elder abuse, and know how and where to report suspected elder abuse (Du Mont et al., 2015).

High-Risk Victims

Persuading older victims to accept services has proven challenging in certain circumstances, for example, in cases in which there is long-standing and repeated abuse (Dunlop, Rothman, Condon, Hebert, & Martinez, 2001; Reeves & Wysong, 2010). Recidivism is thought to be one indicator of a high-risk victim. Therefore, efforts are underway to identify high-risk victims (National Council on Crime and Delinquency, 2013; Sommerfeld, Henderson, Snider, & Aarons, 2014). Once identified, more oversight and resources targeting those individuals is provided (Terracina, Aamodt, & Schillerstrom, 2015).

Eliciting Change in At-Risk Elders

As mentioned previously, one of the most cited risk factors for elder abuse is social isolation (e.g., Acierno et al., 2010), and yet only one intervention has incorporated isolation reduction (Mariam et al., 2015). Using a stages-of-change framework, Eliciting Change in At-Risk Elders (ECARE) is an intervention that aims to reduce or eliminate risk factors while empowering victims through the use of trained outreach specialists—a model that has been successfully used in other fields (DePrince, Labus, Belknap, Buckingham, & Gover, 2012). When victims are reluctant to engage in services, staff actively engage in alliance building. Once an alliance is developed, specialists guide victims using motivational interviewing-type skills to assist older victims in identifying needs, thinking through options, and taking steps toward change. They then connect victims with sustainable services in the community that enhance their safety. These interventions are time consuming and resource intensive. For example, to meet the basic needs of at-risk older adults, outreach specialists may serve as an advocate between older adults and their apartment managers, utility companies, and sometimes financial institutions, as well as helping older adults access additional resources. Mariam et al. (2015) found that a working alliance can be forged with intensely ambivalent older adults (p. 28). The majority of participants (70.9%) made some movement in their change stage.

PRoviding Options To Elderly Clients Together (PROTECT)

The need for depression screening among older adults is gaining prominence (Dong, Simon, Odwazny, & Gorbien, 2008; Roepke-Buehler, Simon, & Dong, 2015). Under the theory that depressive symptoms hamper an older adult's ability to self-protect, Sirey et al. (2015) developed PRoviding

Options To Elderly Clients Together (PROTECT), an intervention desi
to identify elder abuse victims who are experiencing depression or anxiety
and then to offer them treatment designed to alleviate depressive symptoms
and enhance personal resources. PROTECT combines problem-solving
therapy with anxiety management techniques and offers education about
the effect of depressive and anxious symptoms in general, as well as the
potential impact of symptoms on taking steps to resolve the mistreatment.
Women ($N = 68$) were randomly placed in either an elder abuse resolution services combined with PROTECT or a mental health referral group.
Although mental health symptoms were not significantly different at the
16-week follow-up, those in the PROTECT group were more likely to
report having all or most of their needs met, were more satisfied with the
services they received, and had a greater sense of self-efficacy. However,
there was no difference between the two groups in perceived improvement
in the abusive situation.

GUARDIANSHIP AND CONSERVATORSHIP

Guardianship can be conceived of as a preemptive strike against elder
abuse or as an intervention to stop elder abuse that has already occurred.
States differ in their use of the terms *guardian* and *conservator*. As discussed previously, involuntary interventions such as court appointment
of a substitute decision maker (guardianship) are legally authorized in
most states if the client is exposed to a substantial risk of harm or if the
client lacks the capacity to make an informed decision to accept or reject
protective services (Moye & Braun, 2010). Guardianship is governed by
state law (for a review, see Demakis, 2013b) and requires a formal determination of decision-making capacity.[1] A petition is submitted to the court,
and the judge makes a determination regarding capacity. Guardians may
be public programs; private nonprofit or for-profit agencies; individual
professional guardians; attorneys; and perhaps most frequently, family

---

[1] For more information on guardianship state law, visit the website (http://www.americanbar.org/
groups/law_aging/resources/guardianship_law_practice.html) of the American Bar Association
Commission on Law and Aging, "Guardianship Law and Practice."

(see Demakis, 2016, for guidance on interviewing and making recommendations to the court).

of older adults under guardianship is unknown as most lete guardianship data (Wood, 2006); the extent of the nship is also unknown (U.S. Government Accountabil- ity с. . Guardianship monitoring of some form—at least the filing of reports and accountings with the court—is required in all states, although improvements in monitoring have been recommended (Karp & Wood, 2007). Guardianship should be used as a last resort, as it removes fundamental rights (Kohn, 2010; Wright, 2010). However, guardianship can be a necessary solution to elder abuse, offering vital protection for a victim who lacks decision-making capacity. Recent trends are toward limited guardianship in which a guardian has decision-making power only in domains in which the older adult has diminished decision-making capacity, which allows older adults to retain as much decision-making power as possible (Moye, Butz, Marson, Wood, & the ABA-APA Capacity Assessment of Older Adults Working Group, 2007).

INTERVENTIONS FOR ABUSIVE INDIVIDUALS

By statute, APS has had a singular focus on older victims to the exclusion of abusive individuals. More recently, the field has acknowledged the impor- tance of responding to the needs of abusers (Jackson, 2016a; Mosqueda, Burnight, et al., 2016; Pillemer et al., 2015; Reeves & Wysong, 2010). The exclusion of abusers from the elder abuse dialogue disregards the role they play in maintaining abusive relationships (Alon & Berg-Warman, 2014; Henderson, Varble, & Buchanan, 2004). In addition, it has contributed to our lack of empirical understanding of those who abuse older adults (Moore & Browne, 2016). Possible interventions for abusers that have been identified in the literature include counseling and treatment, creating barriers to the victim's finances, respite and assistance, education, criminal justice inter- ventions, limited or no contact with the victim, alternative living arrange- ments, supervised visitation, and vocational training to reduce financial dependency (Breckman & Adelman, 1988; Wolf, 2001). However, no specific program for elder abuse abusers (or its subtypes) has been developed.

CONCLUSION

The two predominant responses to elder abuse have been (a) maintaining the victim–offender relationship by assisting caregivers and (b) separating the victim and offender. As this review reveals, the field is gradually realizing the need to develop interventions that go beyond these dichotomous and limited responses. Elder abuse interventions generally, and interventions focused on mental health specifically, are urgently needed to meet the demand associated with increases in reporting. Clinicians can make an extraordinary contribution to this field by developing mental health interventions that not only assist older adults with recovery but also promote their general well-being and ability to thrive.

Afterword

This book identified numerous gaps in our knowledge of elder abuse. The field has yet to achieve a consensus on a set of definitions, develop thoughtful and useful theories, more carefully identify the consequences associated with elder abuse, and develop interventions. To more effectively intervene in the lives of older Americans, we must fill these and other gaps.

Basic research is needed to understand the underlying causes of elder abuse on which interventions are based. Interventions must incorporate the heterogeneity of both abusers and victims, be specific to the type of abuse involved, and take into consideration the level of victim and abuser culpability and the continuum of complexity among these cases. The field must demand that interventions be evaluated. As is easily discernable, there is a stark absence of interventions for older victims and their abusers. And yet a theme that runs consistently through this book is that older people are deeply attached to their abusers and that the needs of their abusers often take precedence over their own needs (Daniel & Bowes, 2011; Jackson & Hafemeister, 2016). Alternatives to criminal justice interventions are needed because the law generally "works poorly with relationships that continue" (Handler, 1989, p. 543). Programs that work

http://dx.doi.org/10.1037/0000056-007
Understanding Elder Abuse: A Clinician's Guide, by S. L. Jackson

with victims who choose to remain in an abusive relationship must focus on strengthening these interpersonal relationships rather than extinguishing them (Daniel & Bowes, 2011; Henderson, Varble, & Buchanan, 2004; Luo & Waite, 2011; O'Donnell, Treacy, Fealy, Lyons, & Lafferty, 2015). Without addressing these nuances, interventions may be futile, if not harmful. Psychologists stand poised to make a great contribution to this field (S. Wood & Lichtenberg, 2017).

Appendix:
Online Resources

NATIONAL ORGANIZATIONS

Alzheimer's Association: In addition to a website with an abundance of information, there is also a resources locator. http://www.alz.org

American Psychological Association (APA): The APA website has several articles on elder abuse. http://www.apa.org/search.aspx?query=elder%20abuse

Eldercare Locator: The Eldercare Locator connects older Americans and their caregivers with senior services. http://www.eldercare.gov/Eldercare.NET/Public/Index.aspx

National Adult Protective Services Association (NAPSA): NAPSA is a nonprofit organization with a mission to increase the capacity of adult protective services (APS). http://www.napsa-now.org/

National Center on Elder Abuse (NCEA): NCEA serves as a national resource center dedicated to the prevention of elder abuse. https://ncea.acl.gov/

National Clearinghouse on Abuse in Later Life (NCALL): NCALL addresses the nexus between domestic violence, sexual assault, and elder abuse. http://www.ncall.us/

National Council on Aging (NCOA): NCOA facilitates innovative community programs and services, online help, and advocacy. https://www.ncoa.org/

University of California, Irvine, Center of Excellence on Elder Abuse and Neglect: The Center serves as a source of training, technical assistance, research, and policy. http://www.centeronelderabuse.org/about.asp

FEDERAL AGENCIES

National Institute on Aging (NIA): NIA is a leader in aging research, with a newly minted directive to address elder abuse. https://www.nia.nih.gov/

U.S. Department of Health and Human Services, Administration for Community Living, Office of Elder Justice and Adult Protective Services: Housed in the U.S. Department of Health and Human Services, The Office of Elder Justice and Adult Protective Services is the only federal agency dedicated to APS. http://acl.gov/

U.S. Department of Justice, Elder Justice Initiative (EJI): The Elder Justice website provides information and resources for professionals and the general public. https://www.justice.gov/elderjustice

U.S. Department of Justice, Office for Victims of Crime (OVC): OVC provides information, training, and technical assistance to victim assistance professionals. https://www.ovcttac.gov/

U.S. Department of Justice, Office on Violence Against Women (OVW): OVW manages the Enhanced Training and Services to End Abuse in Later Life Program. https://www.justice.gov/ovw

References

Acierno, R., Hernandez, M. A., Amstadter, A. B., Resnick, H. S., Steve, K., Muzzy, W., & Kilpatrick, D. G. (2010). Prevalence and correlates of emotional, physical, sexual, and financial abuse and potential neglect in the United States: The National Elder Mistreatment Study. *American Journal of Public Health, 100,* 292–297. http://dx.doi.org/10.2105/AJPH.2009.163089

Administration on Aging. (2012). *A profile of older Americans: 2012.* Retrieved from Administration for Community Living, U.S. Department of Health and Human Services website: https://www.acl.gov/sites/default/files/Aging%20 and%20Disability%20in%20America/2012profile.pdf

Alon, S., & Berg-Warman, A. (2014). Treatment and prevention of elder abuse and neglect: Where knowledge and practice meet—A model for intervention to prevent and treat elder abuse in Israel. *Journal of Elder Abuse & Neglect, 26,* 150–171. http://dx.doi.org/10.1080/08946566.2013.784087

Alzheimer's Association. (2015). 2015 Alzheimer's disease facts and figures. *Alzheimer's & Dementia: The Journal of the Alzheimer's Association, 11,* 332–384.

American Bar Association Commission on Law and Aging, & American Psychological Association. (2008). *Assessment of older adults with diminished capacity: A handbook for psychologists.* Washington, DC: Author.

American Psychiatric Association. (2013). *Diagnostic and statistical manual of mental disorders* (5th ed.). Washington, DC: Author.

American Psychological Association. (2014). Guidelines for psychological practice with older adults. *American Psychologist, 69,* 34–65. http://www.apa.org/ practice/guidelines/older-adults.pdf

American Psychological Association. (2017). *Ethical principles of psychologists and code of conduct* (2002, Amended June 1, 2010 and January 1, 2017). Retrieved from http://www.apa.org/ethics/code/index.aspx

Amstadter, A. B., Cisler, J. M., McCauley, J. L., Hernandez, M. A., Muzzy, W., & Acierno, R. (2010). Do incident and perpetrator characteristics of elder mistreatment differ by gender of the victim? Results from the National Elder Mistreatment Study. *Journal of Elder Abuse & Neglect, 23*, 43–57. http://dx.doi.org/10.1080/08946566.2011.534707

Amstadter, A. B., Zajac, K., Strachan, M., Hernandez, M. A., Kilpatrick, D. G., & Acierno, R. (2011). Prevalence and correlates of elder mistreatment in South Carolina: The South Carolina elder mistreatment study. *Journal of Interpersonal Violence, 26*, 2947–2972. http://dx.doi.org/10.1177/0886260510390959

Anetzberger, G. (2011). The evolution of a multidisciplinary response to elder abuse. *Marquette Elder's Advisor, 13*(1), 107–128.

Anetzberger, G. J., Korbin, J. E., & Tomita, S. K. (1996). Defining elder mistreatment in four ethnic groups across two generations. *Journal of Cross-Cultural Gerontology, 11*, 187–212. http://dx.doi.org/10.1007/BF00114860

Annotated Laws of Massachusetts, Department of Elder Affairs, ALM GL ch. 19A, § 16(b) (2016).

Aschbrenner, K. A., Greenberg, J. S., Allen, S. M., & Seltzer, M. M. (2010). Subjective burden and personal gains among older parents of adults with serious mental illness. *Psychiatric Services, 61*, 605–611. http://dx.doi.org/10.1176/ps.2010.61.6.605

Ayalon, L., Lev, S., Green, O., & Nevo, U. (2016). A systematic review and meta-analysis of interventions designed to prevent or stop elder maltreatment. *Age and Ageing, 45*, 216–227. http://dx.doi.org/10.1093/ageing/afv193

Bagshaw, D., Wendt, S., Zannettino, L., & Adams, V. (2013). Financial abuse of older people by family members: Views and experiences of older Australians and their family members. *Australian Social Work, 66*(1), 86–103. http://dx.doi.org/10.1080/0312407X.2012.708762

Baladerian, N., & Heisler, C. (2010, November). *Interviewing adults who are elderly and/or have a disability.* Workshop presented at the National Adult Protective Services Association Conference, San Diego, CA.

Balaswamy, S. (2004). Rating of interagency working relationship and associated factors in protective services. *Journal of Elder Abuse & Neglect, 14*, 1–20. http://dx.doi.org/10.1300/J084v14n01_01

Bandura, A. (1973). *Aggression: A social learning analysis.* Oxford, England: Prentice-Hall.

Band-Winterstein, T., Avieli, H., & Smeloy, Y. (2016). Harmed? Harmful? Experiencing abusive adult children with mental disorder over the life course. *Journal of Interpersonal Violence, 31*, 2598–2621.

Barker, J. C. (2002). Neighbors, friends, and other nonkin caregivers of community-living dependent elders. *Journals of Gerontology: Series B. Psychological Sciences and Social Sciences, 57B*(3), S158–S167. https://doi.org/10.1093/geronb/57.3.S158

Barnard, J. W. (2009). Deception, decisions, and investor education. *The Elder Law Journal, 17*, 201–237.

Beach, S. R., Schulz, R., Castle, N. G., & Rosen, J. (2010). Financial exploitation and psychological mistreatment among older adults: Differences between African Americans and non-African Americans in a population-based survey. *The Gerontologist, 50*, 744–757. http://dx.doi.org/10.1093/geront/gnq053

Beach, S. R., Schulz, R., & Sneed, R. (2016). Associations between social support, social networks, and financial exploitation in older adults. *Journal of Applied Gerontology.* Advance online publication. http://dx.doi.org/10.1177/0733464816642584

Beach, S. R., Schulz, R., Williamson, G. M., Miller, L. S., Weiner, M. F., & Lance, C. E. (2005). Risk factors for potentially harmful informal caregiver behavior. *Journal of the American Geriatrics Society, 53*, 255–261. http://dx.doi.org/10.1111/j.1532-5415.2005.53111.x

Beaulaurier, R. L., Seff, L. R., Newman, F. L., & Dunlop, B. D. (2005). Internal barriers to help seeking for middle-aged and older women who experience intimate partner violence. *Journal of Elder Abuse & Neglect, 17*, 53–74. http://dx.doi.org/10.1300/J084v17n03_04

Beaulaurier, R. L., Seff, L. R., Newman, F. L., & Dunlop, B. (2007). External barriers to help seeking for older women who experience intimate partner violence. *Journal of Family Violence, 22*, 747–755. http://dx.doi.org/10.1007/s10896-007-9122-y

Beerman, S., & Markarian, A. M. (2004). *Interviewing techniques for victims of elder abuse who may suffer from Alzheimer's disease or related dementia.* Retrieved from http://www.NYC.gov

Beidler, J. J. (2012). We are family: When elder abuse, neglect, and financial exploitation hit home. *Generations: Journal of the American Society on Aging, 36*(3), 21–25.

Bergeron, L. R. (2000). Servicing the needs of elder abuse victims. *Policy and Practice of Public Human Services, 58*(3), 40–45.

Bergeron, L. R. (2006). Self-determination and elder abuse: Do we know enough? *Journal of Gerontological Social Work, 46*(3/4), 81–102. http://dx.doi.org/10.1300/J083v46n03_05

Bessolo, J. P. (2007, October). Mandatory reporting requirements for financial elder abuse. *Los Angeles Lawyer*, 23–27. Retrieved from https://www.lacba.org/docs/default-source/lal-back-issues/2007-issues/october-2007.pdf

Blum, B. (2015). Forensic evaluations: Testamentary capacity. *The Psychiatric Times, 32*(10), 27–27.

Bond, J. B., Jr., Cuddy, R., Dixon, G. L., Duncan, K. A., & Smith, D. L. (2000). The financial abuse of mentally incompetent older adults: A Canadian study. *Journal of Elder Abuse & Neglect, 11*, 23–38. http://dx.doi.org/10.1300/J084v11n04_03

Bonnie, R. J., & Wallace, R. B. (Eds.). (2003). *Elder mistreatment: Abuse, neglect, and exploitation in an aging America*. Washington, DC: The National Academies Press.

Brandl, B. (2002). Power and control: Understanding domestic abuse in later life. *Generations: Journal of the American Society on Aging, 24*(2), 39–45.

Brandl, B. (2011). *Mandatory reporting of elder abuse: Implications for domestic violence advocates*. Madison, WI: National Clearinghouse on Abuse in Later Life. Retrieved from http://ccerap.org/images/stories/documents/oct-nov-dec-2012/mr-paper-rev-2011.pdf

Brandl, B., Dyer, C. B., Heisler, C. J., Otto, J. M., Stiegel, L. A., & Thomas, R. W. (2007). *Elder abuse detection and intervention: A collaborative approach*. New York, NY: Springer.

Brank, E. M. (2007). Elder research: Filling an important gap in psychology and law. *Behavioral Sciences & the Law, 25*(5), 701–716. http://dx.doi.org/10.1002/bsl.780

Brank, E. M., & Wylie, L. E. (2016). Differing perspectives on older adult caregiving. *Journal of Applied Gerontology, 35*, 698–720. http://dx.doi.org/10.1177/0733464813517506

Brank, E. M., Wylie, L. E., & Hamm, J. A. (2011). Potential for self-reporting of older adult maltreatment: An empirical examination. *The Elder Law Journal, 19*, 351–384.

Breckman, R. S., & Adelman, R. D. (1988). *Strategies for helping victims of elder mistreatment*. Newbury Park, CA: Sage.

Breckman, R., Callahan, J., & Solomon, J. (2015). *Elder abuse multidisciplinary teams: Planning for the future*. New York, NY: New York City Elder Abuse Center.

Brownell, P. (2005). Elder abuse and neglect. In C. N. Dulmus & L. A. Rapp-Paglicci (Eds.), *Handbook of preventive interventions for adults* (pp. 375–394). Hoboken, NJ: Wiley.

Burnes, D. (2016). Community elder mistreatment intervention with capable older adults: Toward a conceptual practice model. *The Gerontologist*, gnv692. http://dx.doi.org/10.1093/geront/gnv692

Burnes, D., Henderson, C. R., Jr., Sheppard, C., Zhao, R., Pillemer, K., & Lachs, M. S. (2017). Prevalence of financial fraud and scams among older adults in the United States: A systematic review and meta-analysis. *American Journal of Public Health, 107*, e13–e21. http://dx.doi.org/10.2105/AJPH.2017.303821

Burnes, D., & Lachs, M. S. (2017). The case for individualized goal attainment scaling measurement in elder abuse interventions. *Journal of Applied Gerontology*, *36*, 116–122. http://dx.doi.org/10.1177/0733464815581486

Burnes, D., Pillemer, K., Caccamise, P. L., Mason, A., Henderson, C. R., Jr., Berman, J., . . . Lachs, M. S. (2015). Prevalence of and risk factors for elder abuse and neglect in the community: A population-based study. *Journal of the American Geriatrics Society*, *63*, 1906–1912. http://dx.doi.org/10.1111/jgs.13601

Burnes, D., Pillemer, K., & Lachs, M. S. (2016). Elder abuse severity: A critical but understudied dimension of victimization for clinicians and researchers. *The Gerontologist*, gnv688. http://dx.doi.org/10.1093/geront/gnv688

Burnes, D. P., Rizzo, V. M., & Courtney, E. (2014). Elder abuse and neglect risk alleviation in protective services. *Journal of Interpersonal Violence*, *29*, 2091–2113. http://dx.doi.org/10.1177/0886260513516387

Burnett, J., Achenbaum, W. A., & Murphy, K. P. (2014). Prevention and early identification of elder abuse. *Clinics in Geriatric Medicine*, *30*, 743–759. http://dx.doi.org/10.1016/j.cger.2014.08.013

Burnett, J., Jackson, S. L., Sinha, A. K., Aschenbrenner, A. R., Murphy, K. P., Xia, R., & Diamond, P. M. (2016). Five-year all-cause mortality rates across five categories of substantiated elder abuse occurring in the community. *Journal of Elder Abuse & Neglect*, *28*, 59–75. http://dx.doi.org/10.1080/08946566.2016.1142920

Burnight, K., & Mosqueda, L. (2011). *Theoretical model development in elder mistreatment.* Washington, DC: National Institute of Justice, Office of Justice Programs, U.S. Department of Justice.

Button, M., Lewis, C., & Tapley, J. (2014). Not a victimless crime: The impact of fraud on individual victims and their families. *Security Journal*, *27*, 36–54. http://dx.doi.org/10.1057/sj.2012.11

California Codes Annotated, Crimes Against Elders, Dependent Adults, and Persons with Disabilities, Cal Pen Code § 368(g) (2017).

Castle, N., Ferguson-Rome, J. C., & Teresi, J. A. (2015). Elder abuse in residential long-term care: An update to the 2003 National Research Council Report. *Journal of Applied Gerontology*, *34*, 407–443.

Centers for Disease Control and Prevention. (2016a). *Elder abuse surveillance: Uniform definitions and recommended core data elements.* Atlanta, GA: National Center for Injury Prevention and Control, Division of Violence Prevention.

Centers for Disease Control and Prevention. (2016b). *Long-term care providers and services users in the United States: Data from the National Study of Long-Term Care Providers, 2013–2014.* Atlanta, GA: National Center for Injury Prevention and Control, Division of Violence Prevention.

Chang, J., & Moon, A. (1997). Korean American elderly's knowledge and perceptions of elder abuse: A qualitative analysis of cultural factors. *Journal of Multicultural Social Work, 6*(1–2), 139–154. http://dx.doi.org/10.1300/J285v06n01_09

Choi, N. G., Kulick, D. B., & Mayer, J. (1999). Financial exploitation of elders: Analysis of risk factors based on county adult protective services data. *Journal of Elder Abuse & Neglect, 10*, 39–62. http://dx.doi.org/10.1300/J084v10n03_03

Choi, N. G., & Mayer, J. (2000). Elder abuse, neglect, and exploitation: Risk factors and prevention strategies. *Journal of Gerontological Social Work, 33*, 5–25. http://dx.doi.org/10.1300/J083v33n02_02

Cisler, J. M., Begle, A. M., Amstadter, A. B., & Acierno, R. (2012). Mistreatment and self-reported emotional symptoms: Results from the National Elder Mistreatment Study. *Journal of Elder Abuse & Neglect, 24*, 216–230. http://dx.doi.org/10.1080/08946566.2011.652923

Clancy, M., McDaid, B., O'Neill, D., & O'Brien, J. G. (2011). National profiling of elder abuse referrals. *Age and Ageing, 40*, 346–352. http://dx.doi.org/10.1093/ageing/afr023

Cohen, M. (2011). Screening tools for the identification of elder abuse. *Journal of Clinical Outcomes Management, 18*, 261–270. Retrieved from http://turner-white.com/pdf/jcom_jun11_abuse.pdf

Cohen, M., Halevi-Levin, S., Gagin, R., & Friedman, G. (2006). Development of a screening tool for identifying elderly people at risk of abuse by their caregivers. *Journal of Aging and Health, 18*(5), 660–685. http://dx.doi.org/10.1177/0898264306293257

Cohn, D., & Taylor, P. (2010). *Baby boomers approach 65—Glumly: Survey findings about America's largest generation.* Pew Research Center, Social & Demographic Trends.

Collins, K. A., & Presnell, S. E. (2006). Elder homicide: A 20-year study. *The American Journal of Forensic Medicine and Pathology, 27*, 183–187. http://dx.doi.org/10.1097/01.paf.0000203268.30433.01

Comijs, H. C., Pot, A. M., Smit, J. H., Bouter, L. M., & Jonker, C. (1998). Elder abuse in the community: Prevalence and consequences. *Journal of the American Geriatrics Society, 46*, 885–888. http://dx.doi.org/10.1111/j.1532-5415.1998.tb02724.x

Connell-Carrick, K., & Scannapieco, M. (2008). Adult protective services: State of the workforce and worker development. *Gerontology & Geriatrics Education, 29*(2), 189–206. http://dx.doi.org/10.1080/02701960802223290

Conrad, K. J., Iris, M., Ridings, J. W., Langley, K., & Wilber, K. H. (2010). Self-report measure of financial exploitation of older adults. *The Gerontologist, 50*, 758–773. http://dx.doi.org/10.1093/geront/gnq054

Conrad, K. J., Iris, M., Ridings, J. W., Rosen, A., Fairman, K. P., & Anetzberger, G. J. (2011). Conceptual model and map of psychological abuse of older adults.

Journal of Elder Abuse & Neglect, 23, 147–168. http://dx.doi.org/10.1080/08946566.2011.558784

Cook, J. M., & Niederehe, G. (2007). Trauma in older adults. In M. J. Friedman, T. M. Keane, & P. A. Resick (Eds.), *Handbook of PTSD: Science and practice* (pp. 252–276). New York, NY: Guilford Press.

Cooper, C., Selwood, A., Blanchard, M., Walker, Z., Blizard, R., & Livingston, G. (2009). Abuse of people with dementia by family carers: Representative cross sectional survey. *BMJ, 338,* b155. http://dx.doi.org/10.1136/bmj.b155

Cooper, C., Selwood, A., & Livingston, G. (2008). The prevalence of elder abuse and neglect: A systematic review. *Age and Ageing, 37,* 151–160. http://dx.doi.org/10.1093/ageing/afm194

Cooper, C., Selwood, A., & Livingston, G. (2009). Knowledge, detection, and reporting of abuse by health and social care professionals: A systematic review. *The American Journal of Geriatric Psychiatry, 17,* 826–838. http://dx.doi.org/10.1097/JGP.0b013e3181b0fa2e

Craik, F. I., & Salthouse, T. A. (Eds.). (2011). *The handbook of aging and cognition.* Hove, England: Psychology Press.

Cramm, J. M., van Dijk, H. M., & Nieboer, A. P. (2013). The importance of neighborhood social cohesion and social capital for the well being of older adults in the community. *The Gerontologist, 53,* 142–152. http://dx.doi.org/10.1093/geront/gns052

Crockett, C., Brandl, B., & Dabby, F. C. (2015). Survivors in the margins: The invisibility of violence against older women. *Journal of Elder Abuse & Neglect, 27,* 291–302. http://dx.doi.org/10.1080/08946566.2015.1090361

Daly, J. M., & Jogerst, G. J. (2014). Multidisciplinary team legislative language associated with elder abuse investigations. *Journal of Elder Abuse & Neglect, 26,* 44–59. http://dx.doi.org/10.1080/08946566.2013.782783

Daniel, B., & Bowes, A. (2011). Re-thinking harm and abuse: Insights from a life-span perspective. *British Journal of Social Work, 41,* 820–836. http://dx.doi.org/10.1093/bjsw/bcq116

Daniels, R. S., Baumhover, L. A., Formby, W. A., & Clark-Daniels, C. L. (1999). Police discretion and elder maltreatment: A nested model of observation, reporting, and satisfaction. *Journal of Criminal Justice, 27,* 209–225. http://dx.doi.org/10.1016/S0047-2352(98)00055-5

D'Aurizio, T. (2007). *Research into community attitudes to elder abuse in Western Australia.* Department for Communities, Government of Western Australia.

Davies, M. L., Gilhooly, M. L., Gilhooly, K. J., Harries, P. A., & Cairns, D. (2013). Factors influencing decision-making by social care and health sector professionals in cases of elder financial abuse. *European Journal of Ageing, 10,* 313–323. http://dx.doi.org/10.1007/s10433-013-0279-3

Davies, M. L., Harries, P. A., Cairns, D., Stanley, D., Gilhooly, M., Gilhooly, K., . . . Hennessy, C. (2011). Factors used in the detection of elder financial abuse: A judgement and decision-making study of social workers and their managers. *Inter-national Social Work, 54,* 404–420. http://dx.doi.org/10.1177/0020872810396256

Davis, R. C., & Medina-Ariza, J. (2001, September). *Results from an elder abuse prevention experiment in New York City* (pp. 1–7). Washington, DC: U.S. Department of Justice, Office of Justice Programs, National Institute of Justice. http://dx.doi.org/10.1037/e528842006-001

Decalmer, P., & Glendenning, F. (1993). *The mistreatment of elderly people* (2nd ed.). London, England: Sage.

Deem, L. D. (2000). Notes from the field: Observations in working with the forgotten victims of personal financial crimes. *Journal of Elder Abuse & Neglect, 12,* 33–48. http://dx.doi.org/10.1300/J084v12n02_05

DeLiema, M., Gassoumis, Z. D., Homeier, D. C., & Wilber, K. H. (2012). Determining prevalence and correlates of elder abuse using promotores: Low-income immigrant Latinos report high rates of abuse and neglect. *Journal of the American Geriatrics Society, 60,* 1333–1339. http://dx.doi.org/10.1111/j.1532-5415.2012.04025.x

DeLiema, M., Navarro, A., Enguidanos, S., & Wilber, K. (2015). Voices from the frontlines: Examining elder abuse from multiple professional perspectives. *Health & Social Work, 40,* e15–e24.

Demakis, G. J. (2012). Adult guardianship. In G. J. Demakis (Ed.), *Civil capacities in clinical neuropsychology: Research findings and practical implications* (pp. 163–184). New York, NY: Oxford University Press.

Demakis, G. J. (2013a). Neuropsychological evaluation of decision-making capacity in older adults. *Psychological Injury and Law, 6,* 41–50. http://dx.doi.org/10.1007/s12207-013-9147-x

Demakis, G. J. (2013b). State statutory definitions of civil incompetency/incapacity: Issues for psychologists. *Psychology, Public Policy, and Law, 19,* 331–342. http://dx.doi.org/10.1037/a0032827

Demakis, G. J. (2016). Evaluating potential guardians for adults adjudicated incompetent. *Archives of Clinical Neuropsychology, 31,* 562–569. http://dx.doi.org/10.1093/arclin/acw047

DeMichele, M. T., Crowe, A., & Stigel, L. A. (2007). Elder abuse: Identifying and responding to probation and parole practices. *Perspectives,* 31–36. Retrieved from http://www.americanbar.org/content/dam/aba/administrative/law_aging/2011_aging_arta2254_prbtaprleprac_tb.authcheckdam.pdf

DePrince, A. P., Labus, J., Belknap, J., Buckingham, S., & Gover, A. (2012). The impact of community-based outreach on psychological distress and victim safety in women exposed to intimate partner abuse. *Journal of Consulting and Clinical Psychology, 80*, 211–221. http://dx.doi.org/10.1037/a0027224

Dessin, C. (2005). Should attorneys have a duty to report financial abuse of the elderly? *Akron Law Review, 38*, 707–723.

de Vries, K. (2013). Communicating with older people with dementia. *Nursing Older People, 25*(4), 30–37. http://dx.doi.org/10.7748/nop2013.05.25.4.30.e429

Doerner, W. G., & Lab, S. P. (2015). *Victimology* (7th ed.). Waltham, MA: Anderson.

Dolon, R., & Blakely, B. (1989). Elder abuse and neglect: A study of adult protective service workers in the United States. *Journal of Elder Abuse & Neglect, 1*(3), 31–50. http://dx.doi.org/10.1300/J084v01n03_04

Dong, X. (2014). Do the definitions of elder mistreatment subtypes matter? Findings from the PINE Study. *The Journals of Gerontology: Series A. Biological Sciences and Medical Sciences, 69*(Suppl. 2), S68–S75. http://dx.doi.org/10.1093/gerona/glu141

Dong, X., Chen, R., & Simon, M. A. (2014). Elder abuse and dementia: A review of the research and health policy. *Health Affairs, 33*, 642–649. http://dx.doi.org/10.1377/hlthaff.2013.1261

Dong, X., & Simon, M. A. (2010). Is impairment in physical function associated with increased risk of elder mistreatment? Findings from a community-dwelling Chinese population. *Public Health Reports*, 743–753.

Dong, X., & Simon, M. A. (2013a). Association between reported elder abuse and rates of admission to skilled nursing facilities: Findings from a longitudinal population-based cohort study. *Gerontology, 59*, 464–472. http://dx.doi.org/10.1159/000351338

Dong, X., & Simon, M. A. (2013b). Elder abuse as a risk factor for hospitalization in older persons. *JAMA Internal Medicine, 173*, 911–917. http://dx.doi.org/10.1001/jamainternmed.2013.238

Dong, X., Simon, M., & Evans, D. (2012). Decline in physical function and risk of elder abuse reported to social services in a community-dwelling population of older adults. *Journal of the American Geriatrics Society, 60*, 1922–1928. http://dx.doi.org/10.1111/j.1532-5415.2012.04147.x

Dong, X., Simon, M., & Evans, D. (2013). Elder self-neglect is associated with increased risk for elder abuse in a community-dwelling population: Findings from the Chicago Health and Aging Project. *Journal of Aging and Health, 25*, 80–96. http://dx.doi.org/10.1177/0898264312467373

Dong, X., Simon, M., Mendes de Leon, C., Fulmer, T., Beck, T., Hebert, L., . . . Evans, D. (2009). Elder self-neglect and abuse and mortality risk in a community-dwelling population. *JAMA, 302*, 517–526. http://dx.doi.org/10.1001/jama.2009.1109

Dong, X., Simon, M. A., Odwazny, R., & Gorbien, M. (2008). Depression and elder abuse and neglect among a community-dwelling Chinese elderly population. *Journal of Elder Abuse & Neglect, 20,* 25–41. http://dx.doi.org/10.1300/J084v20n01_02

Dong, X., Simon, M., Rajan, K., & Evans, D. A. (2011). Association of cognitive function and risk for elder abuse in a community-dwelling population. *Dementia and Geriatric Cognitive Disorders, 32,* 209–215. http://dx.doi.org/10.1159/000334047

Doty, P. (2010). The evolving balance of formal and informal, institutional and non-institutional long-term care for older Americans: A thirty-year perspective. *Public Policy & Aging Report, 20*(1), 3–9. http://dx.doi.org/10.1093/ppar/20.1.3

Dow, B., & Joosten, M. (2012). Understanding elder abuse: A social rights perspective. *International Psychogeriatrics, 24,* 853–855. http://dx.doi.org/10.1017/S1041610211002584

Duke, J. (1997). A national study of involuntary protective services to adult protective services clients. *Journal of Elder Abuse & Neglect, 9*(1), 51–68. http://dx.doi.org/10.1300/J084v09n01_04

Du Mont, J., Kosa, D., Macdonald, S., Elliot, S., & Yaffe, M. (2015). Determining possible professionals and respective roles and responsibilities for a model comprehensive elder abuse intervention: A Delphi consensus survey. *PLoS ONE, 10,* e0140760. Advance online publication. http://dx.doi.org/10.1371/journal.pone.0140760

Dunlop, B. D., Rothman, M. B., Condon, K. M., Hebert, K. S., & Martinez, I. L. (2001). Elder abuse: Risk factors and use of case data to improve policy and practice. *Journal of Elder Abuse & Neglect, 12*(3–4), 95–122. http://dx.doi.org/10.1300/J084v12n03_05

Dutton, D. D. (2006). *Rethinking domestic violence.* Vancouver, British Columbia, Canada: UBC Press.

Dyer, C. B., Heisler, C. J., Hill, C. A., & Kim, L. C. (2005). Community approaches to elder abuse. *Clinics in Geriatric Medicine, 21,* 429–447. http://dx.doi.org/10.1016/j.cger.2004.10.007

Eisikovits, Z., Koren, C., & Band-Winterstein, T. (2013). The social construction of social problems: The case of elder abuse and neglect. *International Psychogeriatrics, 25,* 1291–1298. http://dx.doi.org/10.1017/S1041610213000495

Ekelund, C., Dahlin-Ivanoff, S., & Eklund, K. (2014). Self-determination and older people: A concept analysis. *Scandinavian Journal of Occupational Therapy, 21,* 116–124. http://dx.doi.org/10.3109/11038128.2013.853832

Elder Justice Act, Pub. L. 111-148, 124 Stat. 119 (2009).

Emery, R. E., & Laumann-Billings, L. (1998). An overview of the nature, causes, and consequences of abusive family relationships. Toward differentiating maltreatment and violence. *American Psychologist, 53,* 121–135. http://dx.doi.org/10.1037/0003-066X.53.2.121

Enguidanos, S., DeLiema, M., Aguilar, I., Lambrinos, J., & Wilber, K. (2014). Multicultural voices: Attitudes of older adults in the United States of America about elder mistreatment. *Ageing & Society, 34,* 877–903. http://dx.doi.org/10.1017/S0144686X12001389

Falk, E., & Hoffman, N. (2014). The role of capacity assessments in elder abuse investigations and guardianships. *Clinics in Geriatric Medicine, 30,* 851–868. http://dx.doi.org/10.1016/j.cger.2014.08.009

Fan, R. (1997). Self-determination vs. family-determination: Two incommensurable principles of autonomy. *Bioethics, 11,* 309–322. http://dx.doi.org/10.1111/1467-8519.00070

Feng, J. Y., Fetzer, S., Chen, Y. W., Yeh, L., & Huang, M. C. (2010). Multidisciplinary collaboration reporting child abuse: A grounded theory study. *International Journal of Nursing Studies, 47,* 1483–1490. http://dx.doi.org/10.1016/j.ijnurstu.2010.05.007

Finkel, M. A. (2013). Medical evaluation of child sexual abuse. In R. N. Srivastava, R. Seth, & J. Van Niekerk (Eds.), *Child abuse and neglect: Challenges and opportunities.* New Delhi, India: Jaypee Brothers Medical Publishers.

Fisher, B. S., & Sloan, J. J. (2013). *Campus crime: Legal, social, and policy perspectives.* Springfield, IL: Charles C Thomas.

Fisher, B. S., Zink, T., Pabst, S., Regan, S., & Rinto, B. (2003). Services and programming for older abused women: The Ohio experience. *Journal of Elder Abuse & Neglect, 15,* 67–83. http://dx.doi.org/10.1300/J084v15n02_04

Flint, L. A., Sudore, R. L., & Widera, E. (2012). Assessing financial capacity impairment in older adults. *Generations: Journal of the American Society on Aging, 36*(2), 59–65.

Flores, D. V., Burnett, J., Booker, J., & Dyer, C. (2015, January). *Behind closed doors: Ethnicity, culture, and substance use as risk factors for elder mistreatment.* Paper presented at the Society for Social Work and Research, New Orleans, LA.

Florida Annotated Statutes, Abuse, Neglect, and Exploitation of Elderly Persons and Disabled Adults, Fla. Stat. § 825.101(4) (2017).

Folstein, M. F., Folstein, S. E., & McHugh, P. R. (1975). Mini-mental state: A practical method for grading the cognitive state of patients for the clinician. *Journal of Psychiatric Research, 12,* 189–198.

Friedman, L. S., Avila, S., Tanouye, K., & Joseph, K. (2011). A case-control study of severe physical abuse of older adults. *Journal of the American Geriatrics Society*, *59*, 417–422. http://dx.doi.org/10.1111/j.1532-5415.2010.03313.x

Fulmer, T., Guadagno, L., Dyer, C. B., & Connolly, M. T. (2004). Progress in elder abuse screening and assessment instruments. *Journal of the American Geriatrics Society*, *52*, 297–304. http://dx.doi.org/10.1111/j.1532-5415.2004.52074.x

Fulmer, T., Paveza, G., Abraham, I., & Fairchild, S. (2000). Elder neglect assessment in the emergency department. *Journal of Emergency Nursing*, *26*(5), 436–443. http://dx.doi.org/10.1067/men.2000.110621

Fulmer, T., Paveza, G., VandeWeerd, C., Fairchild, S., Guadagno, L., Bolton-Blatt, M., & Norman, R. (2005). Dyadic vulnerability and risk profiling for elder neglect. *The Gerontologist*, *45*, 525–534. http://dx.doi.org/10.1093/geront/45.4.525

Fulmer, T., Rodgers, R. F., & Pelger, A. (2014). Verbal mistreatment of the elderly. *Journal of Elder Abuse & Neglect*, *26*, 351–364. http://dx.doi.org/10.1080/08946566.2013.801817

Gainey, R. R., & Payne, B. K. (2006). Caregiver burden, elder abuse and Alzheimer's disease: Testing the relationship. *Journal of Health and Human Services Administration*, *29*, 245–259.

Garre-Olmo, J., Planas-Pujol, X., López-Pousa, S., Juvinyà, D., Vilà, A., & Vilalta-Franch, J. (2009). Prevalence and risk factors of suspected elder abuse subtypes in people aged 75 and older. *Journal of the American Geriatrics Society*, *57*, 815–822. http://dx.doi.org/10.1111/j.1532-5415.2009.02221.x

Gassoumis, Z. D., Navarro, A. E., & Wilber, K. H. (2015). Protecting victims of elder financial exploitation: The role of an elder abuse forensic center in referring victims for conservatorship. *Aging & Mental Health*, *19*, 790–798.

Gatz, M., Smyer, M. A., & DiGilio, D. A. (2016). Psychology's contribution to the well-being of older Americans. *American Psychologist*, *71*, 257–267. http://dx.doi.org/10.1037/a0040251

Gerontological Society of America. (2011). *Communicating with older adults: An evidence-based review of what really works.* Retrieved from http://aging.arizona.edu/sites/aging/files/activity_1_reading_1.pdf

Gerstenecker, A., Eakin, A., Triebel, K., Martin, R., Swenson-Dravis, D., Petersen, R. C., & Marson, D. (2016). Age and education corrected older adult normative data for a short form version of the Financial Capacity Instrument. *Psychological Assessment*, *28*, 737–749. http://dx.doi.org/10.1037/pas0000159

Gibbs, L. M. (2014). Understanding the medical markers of elder abuse and neglect: Physical examination findings. *Clinics in Geriatric Medicine*, *30*, 687–712. http://dx.doi.org/10.1016/j.cger.2014.08.002

Gibson, S. C. (2013). *Understanding underreporting of elder financial abuse: Can data support the assumptions* (Doctoral dissertation)? University of Colorado, Colorado Springs. Retrieved from http://hdl.handle.net/10976/260

Gibson, S. C., & Greene, E. (2013). Assessing knowledge of elder financial abuse: A first step in enhancing prosecutions. *Journal of Elder Abuse & Neglect, 25,* 162–182. http://dx.doi.org/10.1080/08946566.2013.751820

Gil, A. P. M., Kislaya, I., Santos, A. J., Nunes, B., Nicolau, R., & Fernandes, A. A. (2015). Elder abuse in Portugal: Findings from the first national prevalence study. *Journal of Elder Abuse & Neglect, 27,* 174–195. http://dx.doi.org/10.1080/08946566.2014.953659

Gillen, M., & Kim, H. (2014). Older adults' receipt of financial help: Does personality matter? *Journal of Family and Economic Issues, 35,* 178–189. http://dx.doi.org/10.1007/s10834-013-9365-0

Glancy, G. D., Ash, P., Bath, E. P., Buchanan, A., Fedoroff, P., Frierson, R. L., . . . Zonana, H. V. (2015). AAPL practice guideline for the forensic assessment. *Journal of the American Academy of Psychiatry and the Law, 43*(2, Suppl.), S3–S53.

Glick, J. B. (2005). Protecting and respecting our elders: Revising mandatory elder abuse reporting statutes to increase efficacy and preserve autonomy. *Virginia Journal of Social Policy & the Law, 12,* 714–743.

Goergen, T., & Beaulieu, M. (2013). Critical concepts in elder abuse research. *International Psychogeriatrics, 25*(8), 1217–1228. http://dx.doi.org/10.1017/S1041610213000501

Gondolf, E. W. (2011). The weak evidence for batterer program alternatives. *Aggression and Violent Behavior, 16,* 347–353. http://dx.doi.org/10.1016/j.avb.2011.04.011

Graves, K., Rosich, R., McBride, M., Charles, G., & LaBelle, J. (2010). Health and health care of Alaska Native older adults. In Periyakoil, V. S. (Ed.), *Ethno Med* (pp. 1–43). Retrieved from http://geriatrics.stanford.edu/wp-content/uploads/downloads/ethnomed/alaskan/downloads/alaska_native.pdf

Greene, A. M., Lepore, M., Lux, L., Porter, K., & Freeland, E. (2015). *Understanding unlicensed care homes: Final report.* Washington, DC: Office of the Assistant Secretary for Planning and Evaluation, U.S. Department of Health and Human Services.

Hagestad, G. O., & Uhlenberg, P. (2005). The social separation of old and young: A root of ageism. *Journal of Social Issues, 61,* 343–360. http://dx.doi.org/10.1111/j.1540-4560.2005.00409.x

Hamby, S., Smith, A., Mitchell, K., & Turner, H. (2016). Poly-victimization and resilience portfolios: Trends in violence research that can enhance the understanding and prevention of elder abuse. *Journal of Elder Abuse & Neglect, 28,* 217–234. http://dx.doi.org/10.1080/08946566.2016.1232182

Handler, J. F. (1989). Community care for the frail elderly: A theory for empowerment. *Ohio State Law Journal, 50,* 541–559.

Harbison, J. R. (2016). *Contesting elder abuse and neglect: Ageism, risk, and the rhetoric of rights in the mistreatment of older people.* Vancouver, British Columbia, Canada: UBC Press.

Harbison, J., Coughlan, S., Karabanow, J., & VanderPlaat, M. (2005). A clash of cultures: Rural values and service delivery to mistreated and neglected older people in Eastern Canada. *Practice, 17,* 229–246. http://dx.doi.org/10.1080/09503150500425091

Hawaii Revised Statutes, Adult Protective Services, § 346-224 (2017).

Heisler, C. (2015, July). *Working with elder abuse clients: How an FJC can help* [Webinar]. Retrieved from https://attendee.gotowebinar.com/recording/9029781392749009154

Heisler, C., & Stiegel, L. A. (2004). Enhancing the justice system's response to elder abuse: Discussions and recommendations of the "Improving Prosecution" working group of the National Policy Summit on Elder Abuse. *Journal of Elder Abuse & Neglect, 14,* 31–54. http://dx.doi.org/10.1300/J084v14n04_05

Helmes, E., & Cuevas, M. (2007). Perceptions of elder abuse among Australian older adults and general practitioners. *Australasian Journal on Ageing, 26,* 120–124. http://dx.doi.org/10.1111/j.1741-6612.2007.00235.x

Henderson, D., Varble, D., & Buchanan, J. A. (2004). Elder abuse: Guidelines for treatment. In W. T. O'Donohue & E. R. Levensky (Eds.), *Handbook of forensic psychology: Resource for mental health and legal professionals* (pp. 743–766). New York, NY: Academic. http://dx.doi.org/10.1016/B978-012524196-0/50031-0

Hershey, D. A., Austin, J. T., & Gutierrez, H. C. (2015). Financial decision making across the adult life span: Dynamic cognitive capacities and real-world competence. In T. M. Hess, J. S., & Lockenhoff, C. E. (Eds.), *Aging and decision making: Empirical and applied perspectives* (pp. 329–349). London, England: Academic Press.

Hillman, J. (2017). Sexual consent capacity: Ethical issues and challenges in long-term care. *Clinical Gerontologist, 40,* 43–50. http://dx.doi.org/10.1080/07317115.2016.1185488

Holtfreter, K., Reisig, M. D., Mears, D. P., & Wolfe, S. E. (2014). *Financial exploitation of the elderly in a consumer context* (Document No. 245388). National Institute of Justice, Office of Justice Programs, U.S. Department of Justice.

Homer, A. C., & Gilleard, C. (1990). Abuse of elderly people by their carers. *BMJ, 301,* 1359–1362. http://dx.doi.org/10.1136/bmj.301.6765.1359

Hooyman, N. R., & Kiyak, H. A. (1988). *Social gerontology: A multidisciplinary perspective*. Boston, MA: Allyn & Bacon.

Horan, M. A., & Clague, J. E. (1999). Injury in the aging: Recovery and rehabilitation. *British Medical Bulletin*, *55*, 895–909. http://dx.doi.org/10.1258/0007142991902709

Howze, K. A., & White, J. L. (2010). Judicial response to elder abuse. *Juvenile & Family Court Journal*, *61*(4), 57–76. http://dx.doi.org/10.1111/j.1755-6988.2010.01048.x

Huddleston, C. (2011, February 28). Managing your parents' money. *Kiplinger*. Retrieved from http://www.kiplinger.com/article/retirement/T066-C000-S002-managing-your-parents-money.html

Hughes, R. B., Lund, E. M., Gabrielli, J., Powers, L. E., & Curry, M. A. (2011). Prevalence of interpersonal violence against community-living adults with disabilities: A literature review. *Rehabilitation Psychology*, *56*, 302–319. http://dx.doi.org/10.1037/a0025620

Hwalek, M. A., Neale, A. V., Goodrich, C. S., & Quinn, K. (1996). The association of elder abuse and substance abuse in the Illinois Elder Abuse System. *The Gerontologist*, *36*, 694–700. http://dx.doi.org/10.1093/geront/36.5.694

Imbody, B., & Vandsburger, E. (2011). Elder abuse and neglect: Assessment tools, interventions, and recommendations for effective service provision. *Educational Gerontology*, *37*, 634–650. http://dx.doi.org/10.1080/15363759.2011.577721

Institute of Medicine. (2014). *Elder abuse and its prevention: Workshop summary*. Forum on Global Violence Prevention, Board on Global Health, Institute of Medicine, National Research Council. Washington, DC: National Academies Press.

Institute of Medicine. (2015). *Cognitive aging: Progress in understanding and opportunities for action*. Washington, DC: The National Academies Press.

Ismail, Z., Rajji, T. K., & Shulman, K. I. (2010). Brief cognitive screening instruments: An update. *International Journal of Geriatric Psychiatry*, *25*, 111–120. http://dx.doi.org/10.1002/gps.2306

Jackson, S. L. (2015a). Elder abuse and neglect. In N. Pachana (Ed.), *Encyclopedia of geropsychology* (pp. 1–7). http://dx.doi.org/10.1007/978-981-287-080-3_192-1

Jackson, S. L. (2015b). The vexing problem of defining financial exploitation. *Journal of Financial Crime*, *22*(1), 63–78. http://dx.doi.org/10.1108/JFC-05-2014-0026

Jackson, S. L. (2016a). All elder abuse perpetrators are not alike: The heterogeneity of elder abuse perpetrators and implications for intervention. *International Journal of Offender Therapy and Comparative Criminology*, *60*, 265–285. http://dx.doi.org/10.1177/0306624X14554063

Jackson, S. L. (2016b). The shifting conceptualization of elder abuse in the United States: From social services, to criminal justice, and beyond. *International Psychogeriatrics*, *28*(1), 1–8. http://dx.doi.org/10.1017/S1041610215001271

Jackson, S. L. (2016c). A systematic review of financial exploitation measures in prevalence studies. *Journal of Applied Gerontology.* Advance online publication. http://dx.doi.org/10.1177/0733464816650801

Jackson, S. L. (2017a). Adult protective services and victim services: A review of the literature to increase understanding between these two fields. *Aggression and Violent Behavior.* Advance online publication. http://dx.doi.org/10.1016/j.avb.2017.01.010

Jackson, S. L. (2017b). GAO reports and senate committee on aging hearings. In X. Dong (Ed.), *Elder abuse: Research, practice, and policy* (pp. 595–613). New York, NY: Springer. http://dx.doi.org/10.1007/978-3-319-47504-2_28

Jackson, S. L., & Hafemeister, T. L. (2010, August). *Financial abuse of elderly people vs. other forms of elder abuse: Assessing their dynamics, risk factors, and society's response.* Final Report to the National Institute of Justice.

Jackson, S. L., & Hafemeister, T. L. (2011). Risk factors associated with elder abuse: The importance of differentiating by type of elder maltreatment. *Violence and Victims, 26,* 738–757. http://dx.doi.org/10.1891/0886-6708.26.6.738

Jackson, S. L., & Hafemeister, T. L. (2012a). APS investigation across four types of elder maltreatment. *Journal of Adult Protection, 14*(2), 82–92. http://dx.doi.org/10.1108/14668201211217530

Jackson, S. L., & Hafemeister, T. L. (2012b). Pure financial exploitation vs. hybrid financial exploitation co-occurring with physical abuse and/or neglect of elderly persons. *Psychology of Violence, 2,* 285–296. http://dx.doi.org/10.1037/a0027273

Jackson, S. L., & Hafemeister, T. L. (2013a). Differences in causal attributions of caseworkers and elderly clients in the USA: Impact on case resolution and cessation of abuse. *Journal of Adult Protection, 15*(5), 1–12. http://dx.doi.org/10.1108/JAP-12-2012-0029

Jackson, S. L., & Hafemeister, T. L. (2013b). Enhancing the safety of elderly victims after the close of an APS investigation. *Journal of Interpersonal Violence, 28*(6), 1223–1239. http://dx.doi.org/10.1177/0886260512468241

Jackson, S. L., & Hafemeister, T. L. (2013c). How do abused elderly persons and their adult protective services caseworkers view law enforcement involvement and criminal prosecution, and what impact do these views have on case processing? *Journal of Elder Abuse & Neglect, 25,* 254–280. http://dx.doi.org/10.1080/08946566.2012.751843

Jackson, S. L., & Hafemeister, T. L. (2013d). *Research in brief: Understanding elder abuse: New directions for developing theories of elder abuse occurring in domestic settings.* Washington, DC: National Institute of Justice, Office of Justice Programs, U.S. Department of Justice. Retrieved from https://www.ncjrs.gov/pdffiles1/nij/241731.pdf

Jackson, S. L., & Hafemeister, T. L. (2014). How case characteristics differ across four types of elder maltreatment: Implications for tailoring interventions to increase victim safety. *Journal of Applied Gerontology, 33,* 982–997. http://dx.doi.org/10.1177/0733464812459370

Jackson, S. L., & Hafemeister, T. L. (2015). The impact of relationship dynamics on the detection and reporting of elder abuse occurring in domestic settings. *Journal of Elder Abuse & Neglect, 27,* 121–145. http://dx.doi.org/10.1080/08946566.2015.1008085

Jackson, S. L., & Hafemeister, T. L. (2016). Theory-based models enhancing the understanding of four types of elder maltreatment. *International Review of Victimology, 22,* 289–320. http://dx.doi.org/10.1177/0269758016630887

Jervis, L. L., Fickenscher, A., Beals, J., & the Shielding American Indian Elders Project Team. (2014). Assessment of elder mistreatment in two American Indian samples: Psychometric characteristics of the HS-EAST and the Native Elder Life–Financial Exploitation and –Neglect measures. *Journal of Applied Gerontology, 33,* 336–356. http://dx.doi.org/10.1177/0733464812470748

Jirik, S., & Sanders, S. (2014). Analysis of elder abuse statutes across the United States, 2011–2012. *Journal of Gerontological Social Work, 57,* 478–497. http://dx.doi.org/10.1080/01634372.2014.884514

Jogerst, G., Daly, J. M., & Ingram, J. (2003). National elder abuse questionnaire: Summary of adult protective service investigator responses. *Journal of Elder Abuse & Neglect, 13,* 59–71. http://dx.doi.org/10.1300/J084v13n04_04

Jogerst, G. J., Dawson, J. D., Hartz, A. J., Ely, J. W., & Schweitzer, L. A. (2000). Community characteristics associated with elder abuse. *Journal of the American Geriatrics Society, 48,* 513–518. http://dx.doi.org/10.1111/j.1532-5415.2000.tb04997.x

Johannesen, M., & LoGiudice, D. (2013). Elder abuse: A systematic review of risk factors in community-dwelling elders. *Age and Ageing, 42,* 292–298. http://dx.doi.org/10.1093/ageing/afs195

Johnson, R. A., & Karlawish, J. (2015). A review of ethical issues in dementia. *International Psychogeriatrics, 27,* 1635–1647. http://dx.doi.org/10.1017/S1041610215000848

Julayanont, P., & Nasreddine, Z. S. (2017). Montreal Cognitive Assessment (MoCA): Concept and clinical review. In A. J. Larner (Ed.), *Cognitive screening instruments* (pp. 139–195). New York, NY: Springer International.

Kahn, J. R., & Pearlin, L. I. (2006). Financial strain over the life course and health among older adults. *Journal of Health and Social Behavior, 47*(1), 17–31. http://dx.doi.org/10.1177/002214650604700102

Kang, J. H., & Lynch, J. P. (2014). Calling the police in instances of family violence: Effects of victim–offender relationship and life stages. *Crime & Delinquency, 60*(1), 34–59. http://dx.doi.org/10.1177/0011128709359655

Kapp, M. B. (1995). Elder mistreatment: Legal interventions and policy uncertainties. *Behavioral Sciences & the Law, 13*, 365–380. http://dx.doi.org/10.1002/bsl.2370130305

Karel, M. J. (2011). Ethics. In V. Molinari (Ed.), *Specialty competencies in geropsychology* (pp. 115–142). New York, NY: Oxford.

Karp, N., & Wood, N. (2007). *Guarding the guardians: Promising practices for court monitoring.* Washington, DC: AARP Public Policy Institute.

Kennedy, R. D. (2005). Elder abuse and neglect: The experience, knowledge, and attitudes of primary care physicians. *Family Medicine, 37*, 481–485.

Klein, A., Tobin, T., Salomon, A., & Dubois, J. (2008). *A statewide profile of older women and the criminal justice response* [Document No. 222459; final report submitted to the National Institute of Justice]. Retrieved from https://www.ncjrs.gov/pdffiles1/nij/grants/222459.pdf

Knight, B. G., Kim, S., Rastegar, S., Jones, S., Jump, V., & Wong, S. (2016). Influences on the perception of elder financial abuse among older adults in Southern California. *International Psychogeriatrics, 28*(1), 163–169. http://dx.doi.org/10.1017/S1041610215000587

Kohn, N. A. (2003). Second childhood: What child protection systems can teach elder protection systems. *Stanford Law & Policy Review, 14*, 175–202.

Kohn, N. A. (2010). Rethinking the constitutionality of age discrimination: A challenge to a decades-old consensus. *U.C. Davis Law Review, 44*, 213–282.

Kohn, N. A. (2012). Elder (In)Justice: A critique of the criminalization of elder abuse. *The American Criminal Law Review, 49*(1), 1–29.

Kohn, N. A. (2014). Vulnerability theory and the role of government. *Yale Journal of Law and Feminism, 26*, 1–27.

Kohout, F. J., Berkman, L. F., Evans, D. A., & Cornoni-Huntley, J. (1993). Two shorter forms of the CES-D depression symptoms index. *Journal of Aging and Health, 5*, 179–193.

Korbin, J. E., Anetzberger, G. J., & Austin, C. (1995). The intergenerational cycle of violence in child and elder abuse. *Journal of Elder Abuse & Neglect, 7*, 1–15. http://dx.doi.org/10.1300/J084v07n01_01

Kosberg, J. I. (2014). Rosalie Wolf Memorial Lecture: Reconsidering assumptions regarding men as elder abuse perpetrators and as elder abuse victims. *Journal of Elder Abuse & Neglect, 26*, 207–222. http://dx.doi.org/10.1080/08946566.2014.898442

Krienert, J. L., Walsh, J. A., & Turner, M. (2009). Elderly in America: A descriptive study of elder abuse examining National Incident-Based Reporting System (NIBRS) data, 2000–2005. *Journal of Elder Abuse & Neglect, 21*, 325–345. http://dx.doi.org/10.1080/08946560903005042

Kurrle, S. (2013). Australia. A. Phelan (Ed.), *International perspectives on elder abuse* (pp. 32–46). New York, NY: Routledge.

Labrum, T. (2017). Factors related to abuse of older persons by relatives with psychiatric disorders. *Archives of Gerontology and Geriatrics, 68,* 126–134. http://dx.doi.org/10.1016/j.archger.2016.09.007

Labrum, T., & Solomon, P. L. (2015). Physical elder abuse perpetrated by relatives with serious mental illness: A preliminary conceptual social–ecological model. *Aggression and Violent Behavior, 25*(Pt. B), 293–303. http://dx.doi.org/10.1016/j.avb.2015.09.006

Lachs, M. S., & Berman, J. (2011). *Under the radar: New York State Elder Abuse Prevalence Study.* New York, NY: William B. Hoyt Memorial New York State Children and Family Trust Fund, New York State Office of Children and Family Services.

Lachs, M. S., & Pillemer, K. A. (2015). Elder Abuse. *The New England Journal of Medicine, 373,* 1947–1956. http://dx.doi.org/10.1056/NEJMra1404688

Larner, A. J. (Ed.). (2017). *Cognitive screening instruments: A practical approach* (2nd ed.). http://dx.doi.org/10.1007/978-3-319-44775-9

Larson, C., & Kao, H. (2016). Caregiving. In J. L. Hayashi & B. Leff (Eds.), *Geriatric home-based medical care* (pp. 269–290). http://dx.doi.org/10.1007/978-3-319-23365-9_13

Lau, Y., & Waite, L. J. (2011). Mistreatment and psychological well-being among older adults: Exploring the role of psychosocial resources and deficits. *The Journals of Gerontology: Series B. Psychological Sciences and Social Sciences, 66,* 217–229.

Laumann, E. O., Leitsch, S. A., & Waite, L. J. (2008). Elder mistreatment in the United States: Prevalence estimates from a nationally representative study. *The Journals of Gerontology: Series B. Psychological Sciences and Social Sciences, 63*(4), S248–S254. http://dx.doi.org/10.1093/geronb/63.4.S248

Le, Q. K. (1998). Mistreatment of Vietnamese elderly by their families in the United States. *Journal of Elder Abuse & Neglect, 9,* 51–62. http://dx.doi.org/10.1300/J084v09n02_05

Lee, Y. S., Kaplan, C. P., & Perez-Stable, E. J. (2014). Elder mistreatment among Chinese and Korean immigrants: The roles of sociocultural contexts on perceptions and help-seeking behaviors. *Journal of Aggression, Maltreatment & Trauma, 23*(1), 20–44. http://dx.doi.org/10.1080/10926771.2014.864741

Lichtenberg, P. A. (2016). The intersection of financial exploitation and financial capacity. *American Psychologist, 71,* 312–320. http://dx.doi.org/10.1037/a0040192

Lichtenberg, P. A., Stoltman, J., Ficker, L. J., Iris, M., & Mast, B. (2015). A person-centered approach to financial capacity assessment: Preliminary development of a new rating scale. *Clinical Gerontologist, 38*(1), 49–67. http://dx.doi.org/ 10.1080/07317115.2014.970318

Lindert, J., de Luna, J., Torres-Gonzales, F., Barros, H., Ioannidi-Kopolou, E., Melchiorre, M. G., ... Soares, J. F. (2013). Abuse and neglect of older persons in seven cities in seven countries in Europe: A cross-sectional community study. *International Journal of Public Health, 58*, 121–132. http://dx.doi.org/10.1007/ s00038-012-0388-3

Lindert, J., Luna, J., Torres-Gonzalez, F., Barros, H., Ioannidi-Kapolou, E., Quattrini, S., ... Soares, J. J. (2012). Study design, sampling and assessment methods of the European study 'Abuse of the elderly in the European region.' *European Journal of Public Health, 22*, 662–666. http://dx.doi.org/10.1093/ eurpub/ckr079

Lindland, E., Fond, M., Haydon, A., & Kendall-Taylor, N. (2015). *Gauging aging: Mapping the gaps between expert and public understandings of aging in America.* Washington, DC: FrameWorks Institute.

Lithwick, M., Beaulieu, M., Gravel, S., & Straka, S. M. (1999). The mistreatment of older adults: Perpetrator–victim relationships and interventions. *Journal of Elder Abuse & Neglect, 11*, 95–112.

Little, J. T., Satlin, A., Sunderland, T., & Volicer, L. (1995). Sundown syndrome in severely demented patients with probable Alzheimer's disease. *Journal of Geriatric Psychiatry and Neurology, 8*, 103–106. http://dx.doi.org/10.1177/ 089198879500800205

LoFaso, V. M., & Rosen, T. (2014). Medical and laboratory indicators of elder abuse and neglect. *Clinics in Geriatric Medicine, 30*, 713–728. http://dx.doi.org/ 10.1016/j.cger.2014.08.003

Lowndes, G., Darzins, P., Wainer, J., Owada, K., & Mihaljcic, T. (2009). *Financial abuse of elders: A review of the evidence: Protecting Elders Assets Study.* Victoria, Australia: Monash Institute of Health Services Research, Faculty of Medicine, Nursing and Health Sciences.

Luescher, K., & Pillemer, K. (1998). Intergenerational ambivalence: A new approach to the study of parent–child relations in later life. *Journal of Marriage and the Family, 60*, 413–425. http://dx.doi.org/10.2307/353858

Luo, Y., & Waite, L. J. (2011). Mistreatment and psychological well-being among older adults: Exploring the role of psychosocial resources and deficits. *The Journals of Gerontology: Series B. Psychological Sciences and Social Sciences, 66*, 217–229. http://dx.doi.org/10.1093/geronb/gbq096

Macassa, G., Viitasara, E., Sundin, Ö., Barros, H., Torres Gonzales, F., Ioannidi-Kapolou, E., ... Soares, J. J. (2013). Psychological abuse among older persons in Europe: A cross-sectional study. *Journal of Aggression, Conflict and Peace Research, 5*(1), 16–34. http://dx.doi.org/10.1108/17596591311290722

Maccoby, E. E. (2000). The uniqueness of parent–child relationships. In W. A. Collins & B. Laursen (Eds.), *The Minnesota Symposia on Child Development: Vol. 30. Relationships as developmental contexts* (pp. 157–175). Mahwah, NJ: Erlbaum.

Macy, R. J., Giattina, M., Sangster, T. H., Crosby, C., & Montijo, N. J. (2009). Domestic violence and sexual assault services: Inside the black box. *Aggression and Violent Behavior, 14,* 359–373. http://dx.doi.org/10.1016/j.avb.2009.06.002

Manning, C. A., & Ducharme, J. K. (2010). Dementia syndromes in the older adult. In P. A. Lichtenberg (Ed.), *Handbook of assessment in clinical gerontology* (2nd ed., pp. 155–178). http://dx.doi.org/10.1016/B978-0-12-374961-1.10006-5

Marett, C. P., & Mossman, D. (2015). Autonomy vs. abuse: Can a patient choose a new power of attorney? *Current Psychiatry, 14*(3), 37–40.

Mariam, L. M., McClure, R., Robinson, J. B., & Yang, J. A. (2015). Eliciting change in at-risk elders (ECARE): Evaluation of an elder abuse intervention program. *Journal of Elder Abuse & Neglect, 27,* 19–33. http://dx.doi.org/10.1080/08946566.2013.867241

Marson, D. C., Hebert, K., & Solomon, A. C. (2011). Assessing civil competencies in older adults with dementia. In G. J. Larrabee (Ed.), *Forensic neuropsychology: A scientific approach* (pp. 401–437). New York, NY: Oxford University Press.

Marson, D. C., Martin, R. C., Wadley, V., Griffith, H. R., Snyder, S., Goode, P. S., . . . Harrell, L. E. (2009). Clinical interview assessment of financial capacity in older adults with mild cognitive impairment and Alzheimer's disease. *Journal of the American Geriatrics Society, 57,* 806–814. http://dx.doi.org/10.1111/j.1532-5415.2009.02202.x

Marson, D. C., Sawrie, S. M., Snyder, S., McInturff, B., Stalvey, T., Boothe, A., . . . Harrell, L. E. (2000). Assessing financial capacity in patients with Alzheimer disease: A conceptual model and prototype instrument. *Archives of Neurology, 57,* 877–884. http://dx.doi.org/10.1001/archneur.57.6.877

Mast, B. T., & Gerstenecker, A. (2010). Screening instruments and brief batteries for dementia. In P. A. Lichtenberg (Ed.), *Handbook of assessment in clinical gerontology* (pp. 503–530). http://dx.doi.org/10.1016/B978-0-12-374961-1.10019-3

Mastin, T., Choi, J., Barboza, G. E., & Post, L. (2007). Newspapers' framing of elder abuse: It's not a family affair. *Journalism & Mass Communication Quarterly, 84,* 777–794. http://dx.doi.org/10.1177/107769900708400408

McCart, M. R., Smith, D. W., & Sawyer, G. K. (2010). Help seeking among victims of crime: A review of the empirical literature. *Journal of Traumatic Stress, 23,* 198–206.

Melchiorre, M. G., Chiatti, C., Lamura, G., Torres-Gonzales, F., Stankunas, M., Lindert, J., . . . Soares, J. F. (2013). Social support, socio-economic status, health and abuse among older people in seven European countries. *PLoS ONE, 8*(1), e54856. http://dx.doi.org/10.1371/journal.pone.0054856

Meirson, A. (2008). Prosecuting elder abuse: Setting the gold standard in the Golden State. *The Hastings Law Journal, 60,* 431–452.

Mihaljcic, T., & Lowndes, G. (2013). Individual and community attitudes toward financial elder abuse. *Journal of Elder Abuse & Neglect, 25,* 183–203. http://dx.doi.org/10.1080/08946566.2012.712867

Millán-Calenti, J. C., Tubío, J., Pita-Fernández, S., González-Abraldes, I., Lorenzo, T., Fernández-Arruty, T., & Maseda, A. (2010). Prevalence of functional disability in activities of daily living (ADL), instrumental activities of daily living (IADL) and associated factors, as predictors of morbidity. *Archives of Gerontology and Geriatrics, 50,* 306–310. http://dx.doi.org/10.1016/j.archger.2009.04.017

Miller, B. (1995). Autonomia. In W. T. Reich (Ed.), *Encyclopedia of bioethics* (Rev. ed.). New York, NY: MacMillan.

Mills, W. L., Roush, R. E., Moye, J., Kunik, M. E., Wilson, N. L., Taffet, G. E., & Naik, A. D. (2012). An educational program to assist clinicians in identifying elder investment fraud and financial exploitation. *Gerontology & Geriatrics Education, 33,* 351–363. http://dx.doi.org/10.1080/02701960.2012.702164

Mitchell, A. J. (2009). A meta-analysis of the accuracy of the mini-mental state examination in the detection of dementia and mild cognitive impairment. *Journal of Psychiatric Research, 43,* 411–431. http://dx.doi.org/10.1016/j.jpsychires.2008.04.014

Moon, A., Tomita, S. K., & Jung-Kamei, S. (2002). Elder mistreatment among four Asian American groups: An exploratory study on tolerance, victim blaming and attitudes toward third-party intervention. *Journal of Gerontological Social Work, 36*(1–2), 153–169. http://dx.doi.org/10.1300/J083v36n01_09

Moon, A., & Williams, O. (1993). Perceptions of elder abuse and help-seeking patterns among African-American, Caucasian American, and Korean-American elderly women. *The Gerontologist, 33,* 386–395. http://dx.doi.org/10.1093/geront/33.3.386

Moore, C., & Browne, C. (2016). Emerging innovations, best practices, and evidence-based practices in elder abuse and neglect: A review of recent developments in the field. *Journal of Family Violence,* 1–15.

Morgan, R. E., & Mason, B. J. (2014). *Crimes against the elderly, 2003–2013* (NCJ 248339). Washington, DC: Bureau of Justice Statistics, Office of Justice Programs, U.S. Department of Justice.

Morris, J. R. (2010). The Bet Tzedek legal services model: How a legal services model addresses elder abuse and neglect. *Journal of Elder Abuse & Neglect, 22,* 275–280. http://dx.doi.org/10.1080/08946566.2010.490139

Moskowitz, S., & DeBoer, M. J. (1999). When silence resounds: Clergy and the requirement to report elder abuse and neglect. *De Paul Law Review, 49,* 1–83.

Mosqueda, L. (2013). *Geriatric pocket doc: A resource for non-physicians.* Irvine: University of California Irvine.

Mosqueda, L., Burnight, K., Gironda, M. W., Moore, A. A., Robinson, J., & Olsen, B. (2016). The abuse intervention model: A pragmatic approach to intervention for elder mistreatment. *Journal of the American Geriatrics Society, 64,* 1879–1883. http://dx.doi.org/10.1111/jgs.14266

Mosqueda, L., Burnight, K., & Liao, S. (2005). The life cycle of bruises in older adults. *Journal of the American Geriatrics Society, 53*(8), 1339–1343. http://dx.doi.org/10.1111/j.1532-5415.2005.53406.x

Mosqueda, L., & Olsen, B. (2015). Elder abuse and neglect. In P. A. Lichtenberg & B. T. Mast (Eds.), *APA handbook of clinical geropsychology: Vol. 2. Assessment, treatment, and issues of later life* (pp. 667–686). http://dx.doi.org/10.1037/14459-026

Mosqueda, L., Wiglesworth, A., Moore, A. A., Nguyen, A., Gironda, M., & Gibbs, L. (2016). Variability in findings from adult protective services investigations of elder abuse in California. *Journal of Evidence-Informed Social Work, 13*(1), 34–44. http://dx.doi.org/10.1080/15433714.2014.939383

Mouton, C. P., Larme, A. C., Alford, C. L., Talamantes, M. A., McCorkle, R. J., & Burge, S. K. (2005). Multiethnic perspectives on elder mistreatment. *Journal of Elder Abuse & Neglect, 17,* 21–44. http://dx.doi.org/10.1300/J084v17n02_02

Mouton, C. P., Rodabough, R. J., Rovi, S. L., Hunt, J. L., Talamantes, M. A., Brzyski, R. G., & Burge, S. K. (2004). Prevalence and 3-year incidence of abuse among postmenopausal women. *American Journal of Public Health, 94,* 605–612. http://dx.doi.org/10.2105/AJPH.94.4.605

Moye, J., & Braun, M. (2010). Assessment of capacity. In P. Lichtenberg (Ed.), *Handbook of assessment in clinical gerontology* (pp. 581–618). http://dx.doi.org/10.1016/B978-0-12-374961-1.10022-3

Moye, J., Butz, S. W., Marson, D. C., Wood, E., & the ABA-APA Capacity Assessment of Older Adults Working Group. (2007). A conceptual model and assessment template for capacity evaluation in adult guardianship. *The Gerontologist, 47,* 591–603. http://dx.doi.org/10.1093/geront/47.5.591

Moye, J., & Marson, D. C. (2007). Assessment of decision-making capacity in older adults: An emerging area of practice and research. *The Journals of Gerontology: Series B. Psychological Sciences and Social Sciences, 62*(1), P3–P11. http://dx.doi.org/10.1093/geronb/62.1.P3

Moyer, V. A., & the U.S. Preventive Services Task Force. (2013). Screening for intimate partner violence and abuse of elderly and vulnerable adults: U.S. Preventive

Services Task Force recommendation statement. *Annals of Internal Medicine,* *158,* 478–486. http://dx.doi.org/10.7326/0003-4819-158-6-201303190-00588

Moyer, V. A., & the U.S. Preventive Services Task Force. (2014). Screening for cognitive impairment in older adults: U.S. Preventive Services Task Force recommendation statement. *Annals of Internal Medicine, 160,* 791–797. http://dx.doi.org/10.7326/M14-0496

Murphy, K., Waa, S., Jaffer, H., Sauter, A., & Chan, A. (2013). A literature review of findings in physical elder abuse. *Canadian Association of Radiologists Journal,* *64*(1), 10–14. http://dx.doi.org/10.1016/j.carj.2012.12.001

Mysyuk, Y., Westendorp, R. G. J., & Lindenberg, J. (2013). Added value of elder abuse definitions: A review. *Ageing Research Reviews, 12*(1), 50–57. http://dx.doi.org/10.1016/j.arr.2012.04.001

Naik, A. D., Lai, J. M., Kunik, M. E., & Dyer, C. B. (2008). Assessing capacity in suspected cases of self-neglect. *Geriatrics, 63*(2), 24–31.

National Adult Protective Services Association. (2015). *Code of ethics.* Retrieved from http://www.napsa-now.org/about-napsa/code-of-ethics/

National Council on Crime and Delinquency. (2013, October). *Data-informed practice: How Texas is developing and implementing the structured decision making model.* Presentation at the 24th Annual NAPSA Conference, St. Paul, MN.

National Institute of Justice. (2014). *Elder mistreatment: Using theory in research* [Meeting summary]. Washington, DC: National Institute of Justice, Office of Justice Programs, U.S. Department of Justice.

Naughton, C., Drennan, J., & Lafferty, A. (2014). Older people's perceptions of the term elder abuse and characteristics associated with a lower level of awareness. *Journal of Elder Abuse & Neglect, 26,* 300–318. http://dx.doi.org/10.1080/08946566.2013.867242

Naughton, C., Drennan, J., Lyons, I., Lafferty, A., Treacy, M., Phelan, A., . . . Delaney, L. (2012). Elder abuse and neglect in Ireland: Results from a national prevalence survey. *Age and Ageing, 41,* 98–103. http://dx.doi.org/10.1093/ageing/afr107

Navarro, A. E., Gassoumis, Z. D., & Wilber, K. H. (2013). Holding abusers accountable: An elder abuse forensic center increases criminal prosecution of financial exploitation. *The Gerontologist, 53,* 303–312. http://dx.doi.org/10.1093/geront/gns075

Neale, A. V., Hwalek, M. A., Scott, R. O., Sengstock, M. C., & Stahl, C. (1991). Validation of the Hwalek-Sengstock Elder Abuse Screening Test. *Journal of Applied Gerontology, 10,* 406–418. http://dx.doi.org/10.1177/073346489101000403

Nerenberg, L. (2008). *Elder abuse prevention: Emerging trends and promising strategies.* New York, NY: Springer.

Newmark, L. (2006). *Crime victims' needs and VOCA-funded services: Findings and recommendations from two national studies* (Document No. 214263). Washington, DC: National Institute of Justice, Office of Justice Programs, U.S. Department of Justice.

Nievod, A. (1992). Undue influence in contract and probate law. *Journal of Questioned Document Examination, 1*, 14–26.

O'Connor, D., Hall, M. I., & Donnelly, M. (2009). Assessing capacity within a context of abuse or neglect. *Journal of Elder Abuse & Neglect, 21*, 156–169. http://dx.doi.org/10.1080/08946560902779993

O'Donnell, D., Phelan, A., & Fealy, G. (2015). *Interventions and services which address elder abuse: An integrated review.* Dublin, Ireland: National Centre for the Protection of Older People, University College Dublin.

O'Donnell, D., Treacy, M. P., Fealy, G., Lyons, I., & Lafferty, A. (2015). The case management approach to protecting older people from abuse and mistreatment: Lessons from the Irish experience. *British Journal of Social Work, 45*, 1451–1468. http://dx.doi.org/10.1093/bjsw/bcu027

Office for Victims of Crime. (2011). *Victims with disabilities: The forensic interview— Techniques for interviewing victims with communication and/or cognitive disabilities* [DVD and guidebook]. Available from https://ovc.ncjrs.gov/Publications.aspx?SeriesID=43

Ogle, C. M., Rubin, D. C., & Siegler, I. C. (2013). The impact of the developmental timing of trauma exposure on PTSD symptoms and psychosocial functioning among older adults. *Developmental Psychology, 49*(11), 2191–2200. http://dx.doi.org/10.1037/a0031985

Oh, J., Kim, H. S., Martins, D., & Kim, H. (2006). A study of elder abuse in Korea. *International Journal of Nursing Studies, 43*(2), 203–214. http://dx.doi.org/10.1016/j.ijnurstu.2005.03.005

O'Keeffe, M., Hills, A., Doyle, M., McCreadie, C., Scholes, S. Y., Constantine, R., . . . Erens, B. (2007). *UK Study of abuse and neglect of older People: Prevalence study report.* London, England: National Centre for Social Research, King's College London.

Okonkwo, O. C., Wadley, V. G., Griffith, H. R., Belue, K., Lanza, S., Zamrini, E. Y., . . . Marson, D. C. (2008). Awareness of deficits in financial abilities in patients with mild cognitive impairment: Going beyond self-informant discrepancy. *The American Journal of Geriatric Psychiatry, 16*, 650–659. http://dx.doi.org/10.1097/JGP.0b013e31817e8a9d

Parra-Cardona, J. R., Meyer, E., Schiamberg, L., & Post, L. (2007). Elder abuse and neglect in Latino families: An ecological and culturally relevant theoretical framework for clinical practice. *Family Process, 46*, 451–470. http://dx.doi.org/10.1111/j.1545-5300.2007.00225.x

Parton, N. (1979). The natural history of child abuse: A study in social problem definition. *British Journal of Social Work, 9*, 431–451.

Payne, B. K. (2002). An integrated understanding of elder abuse and neglect. *Journal of Criminal Justice, 30*, 535–547. http://dx.doi.org/10.1016/S0047-2352(02)00175-7

Payne, B. K. (2011). *Crime and elder abuse: An integrated perspective* (3rd ed.). Springfield, IL: Charles C Thomas.

Payne, B. K., & Berg, B. L. (2003). Perceptions about the criminalization of elder abuse among police chiefs and ombudsmen. *Crime & Delinquency, 49*, 439–459. http://dx.doi.org/10.1177/0011128703049003005

Payne, B. K., Berg, B. L., & Toussaint, J. (2001). The police response to the criminalization of elder abuse: An exploratory study. *Policing: An International Journal of Police Strategies & Management, 24*, 605–626. http://dx.doi.org/10.1108/EUM0000000006500

Payne, B. K., & Gainey, R. R. (2005). Differentiating self-neglect as a type of elder mistreatment: How do these cases compare to traditional types of elder mistreatment? *Journal of Elder Abuse & Neglect, 17*, 21–36. http://dx.doi.org/10.1300/J084v17n01_02

Penhale, B. (2003). Older women, domestic violence, and elder abuse: A review of commonalities, differences, and shared approaches. *Journal of Elder Abuse & Neglect, 15*, 163–183. http://dx.doi.org/10.1300/J084v15n03_10

Penhale, B. (2010). Responding and intervening in elder abuse and neglect. *Ageing International, 35*, 235–252. http://dx.doi.org/10.1007/s12126-010-9065-0

Petersen, R. C., Caracciolo, B., Brayne, C., Gauthier, S., Jelic, V., & Fratiglioni, L. (2014). Mild cognitive impairment: A concept in evolution. *Journal of Internal Medicine, 275*, 214–228. http://dx.doi.org/10.1111/joim.12190

Peterson, J. C., Burnes, D. P., Caccamise, P. L., Mason, A., Henderson, C. R., Jr., Wells, M. T., . . . Lachs, M. S. (2014). Financial exploitation of older adults: A population-based prevalence study. *Journal of General Internal Medicine, 29*, 1615–1623. http://dx.doi.org/10.1007/s11606-014-2946-2

Phelan, A. (2008). Elder abuse, ageism, human rights and citizenship: Implications for nursing discourse. *Nursing Inquiry, 15*, 320–329. http://dx.doi.org/10.1111/j.1440-1800.2008.00423.x

Phelan, A. (Ed.). (2013). *International perspectives on elder abuse*. New York, NY: Routledge.

Pillemer, K. (2005). Abuse is caused by deviance and dependence of caregivers. In D. R. Loseke, R. J. Gelles, & M. M. Cavanaugh (Eds.), *Current controversies on family violence* (2nd ed., pp. 207–220). http://dx.doi.org/10.4135/9781483328584.n13

Pillemer, K., Connolly, M. T., Breckman, R., Spreng, N., & Lachs, M. S. (2015). Elder mistreatment: Priorities for consideration by the White House Conference on Aging. *The Gerontologist, 55,* 320–327. http://dx.doi.org/10.1093/geront/gnu180

Pillemer, K. A., Mueller-Johnson, K. U., Mock, S. E., Suitor, J. J., & Lachs, M. S. (2007). Interventions to prevent elder mistreatment. In L. S. Doll, S. E. Bonzo, D. A. Sleet, & J. A. Mercy (Eds.), *Handbook of injury and violence prevention* (pp. 241–254). http://dx.doi.org/10.1007/978-0-387-29457-5_13

Pinquart, M., & Sörensen, S. (2003). Associations of stressors and uplifts of caregiving with caregiver burden and depressive mood: A meta-analysis. *The Journals of Gerontology: Series B. Psychological Sciences and Social Sciences, 58*(2), 112–128. http://dx.doi.org/10.1093/geronb/58.2.P112

Pinsker, D. M., Pachana, N. A., Wilson, J., Tilse, C., & Byrne, G. J. (2010). Financial capacity in older adults: A review of clinical assessment approaches and considerations. *Clinical Gerontologist, 33,* 332–346. http://dx.doi.org/10.1080/07317115.2010.502107

Pisani, L. D., & Walsh, C. A. (2012). Screening for elder abuse in hospitalized older adults with dementia. *Journal of Elder Abuse & Neglect, 24,* 195–215. http://dx.doi.org/10.1080/08946566.2011.652919

Plaisance, L. Q. (2008). Will you still . . . When I'm sixty-four: Adult children's legal obligations to aging parents. *Journal of the American Academy of Matrimonial Lawyers, 21,* 245–270.

Plassman, B. L., Langa, K. M., Fisher, G. G., Heeringa, S. G., Weir, D. R., Ofstedal, M. B., . . . Wallace, R. B. (2007). Prevalence of dementia in the United States: The aging, demographics, and memory study. *Neuroepidemiology, 29,* 125–132. http://dx.doi.org/10.1159/000109998

Plassman, B. L., Langa, K. M., Fisher, G. G., Heeringa, S. G., Weir, D. R., Ofstedal, M. B., . . . Wallace, R. B. (2008). Prevalence of cognitive impairment without dementia in the United States. *Archives of Internal Medicine, 148,* 427–434.

Podnieks, E. (1992). National survey on abuse of the elderly in Canada. *Journal of Elder Abuse & Neglect, 4,* 5–58.

Policastro, C., Gainey, R., & Payne, B. K. (2015). Conceptualizing crimes against older persons: Elder abuse, domestic violence, white-collar offending, or just regular 'old' crime. *Journal of Criminal Justice, 38,* 27–41.

Polivka, L. (2012). A future out of reach? The growing risk in the U.S. retirement security system. *Generations: Journal of the American Society on Aging, 36*(2), 12–17.

Price, T., King, P. S., Dillard, R. L., & Bulot, J. J. (2011). Elder financial exploitation: Implications for future policy and research in elder mistreatment. *The Western Journal of Emergency Medicine, 12,* 354–356.

Prince, M., Bryce, R., Albanese, E., Wimo, A., Ribeiro, W., & Ferri, C. P. (2013). The global prevalence of dementia: A systematic review and metaanalysis. *Alzheimer's & Dementia, 9*(1), 63–75.e2. http://dx.doi.org/10.1016/j.jalz.2012.11.007

Quinn, K. (2013, February). *2012 survey of adult protective services agencies throughout the country.* Unpublished report.

Quinn, K., & Zielke, H. (2005). Elder abuse, neglect, and exploitation: Policy issues. *Clinics in Geriatric Medicine, 21,* 449–457. http://dx.doi.org/10.1016/j.cger.2005.01.002

Quinn, K. M., & Benson, W. F. (2012). The states' elder abuse victim services: A system still in search of support. *Generations: Journal of the American Society on Aging, 36*(3), 66–72.

Reeves, S., & Wysong, J. (2010). Strategies to address financial abuse. *Journal of Elder Abuse & Neglect, 22,* 328–334. http://dx.doi.org/10.1080/08946566.2010.490182

Regan, J. J. (1981). Protecting the elderly: The new paternalism. *The Hastings Law Journal, 32,* 1111–1132.

Reis, M., & Nahmiash, D. (1995). When seniors are abused: An intervention model. *The Gerontologist, 35,* 666–671. http://dx.doi.org/10.1093/geront/35.5.666

Reis, M., & Nahmiash, D. (1998). Validation of the Indicators of Abuse (IOA) screen. *The Gerontologist, 38,* 471–480. http://dx.doi.org/10.1093/geront/38.4.471

Riggs, D. S., & O'Leary, K. D. (1989). A theoretical model of courtship aggression. In M. A. Pirog-Good & J. E. Stets (Eds.), *Violence in dating relationships: Emerging social issues* (pp. 53–71). New York, NY: Praeger.

Roberto, K. A. (2016). The complexities of elder abuse. *American Psychologist, 71,* 302–311. http://dx.doi.org/10.1037/a0040259

Roberts, R. O., Knopman, D. S., Mielke, M. M., Cha, R. H., Pankratz, V. S., Christianson, T. J., . . . Petersen, R. C. (2014). Higher risk of progression to dementia in mild cognitive impairment cases who revert to normal. *Neurology, 82,* 317–325. http://dx.doi.org/10.1212/WNL.0000000000000055

Roepke-Buehler, S. K., Simon, M., & Dong, X. (2015). Association between depressive symptoms, multiple dimensions of depression, and elder abuse: A cross-sectional, population-based analysis of older adults in urban Chicago. *Journal of Aging and Health, 27,* 1003–1025. http://dx.doi.org/10.1177/0898264315571106

Rom-Rymer, B. N. (2006). Forensic psychology: Emerging topics and expanding roles. In A. M. Goldstein (Ed.), *Forensic psychology: Emerging topics and expanding roles* (pp. 633–660). Hoboken, NJ: Wiley.

Rusbult, C. E., & Van Lange, P. A. (2003). Interdependence, interaction, and relationships. *Annual Review of Psychology, 54,* 351–375. http://dx.doi.org/10.1146/annurev.psych.54.101601.145059

Russo, A. C., Bush, S. S., & Rasin-Waters, D. (2013). Ethical considerations in the neuropsychological assessment of older adults. In L. D. Ravdin & H. L. Katzen (Eds.), *Handbook on the neuropsychology of aging and dementia* (pp. 225–235). http://dx.doi.org/10.1007/978-1-4614-3106-0_15

Sanders, A. E. (2016). Caregiver stress and the patient with dementia. *CONTINUUM: Lifelong Learning in Neurology, 22,* 619–625.

Sapolsky, R., Armanini, M., Packan, D., & Tombaugh, G. (1987). Stress and glucocorticoids in aging. *Endocrinology and Metabolism Clinics of North America, 16,* 965–980.

Schafer, M. H., & Koltai, J. (2014). Does embeddedness protect? Personal network density and vulnerability to mistreatment among older American adults. *The Journals of Gerontology: Series B. Psychological Sciences and Social Sciences, 70,* 597–606. http://dx.doi.org/10.1093/geronb/gbu071

Scheiderer, E. M. (2012). Elder abuse: Ethical and related considerations for professionals in psychology. *Ethics & Behavior, 22*(1), 75–87. http://dx.doi.org/10.1080/10508422.2012.638828

Schiamberg, L. B., & Gans, D. (2000). Elder abuse by adult children: An applied ecological framework for understanding contextual risk factors and the intergenerational character of quality of life. *The International Journal of Aging & Human Development, 50,* 329–359. http://dx.doi.org/10.2190/DXAX-8TJ9-RG5K-MPU5

Schmeidel, A. N., Daly, J. M., Rosenbaum, M. E., Schmuch, G. A., & Jogerst, G. J. (2012). Health care professionals' perspectives on barriers to elder abuse detection and reporting in primary care settings. *Journal of Elder Abuse & Neglect, 24,* 17–36. http://dx.doi.org/10.1080/08946566.2011.608044

Schofield, M. J., & Mishra, G. D. (2003). Validity of self-report screening scale for elder abuse: Women's Health Australia Study. *The Gerontologist, 43,* 110–120. http://dx.doi.org/10.1093/geront/43.1.110

Setterlund, D., Tilse, C., Wilson, J., McCawley, A.-L., & Rosenman, L. (2007). Understanding financial elder abuse in families: The potential of routine activities theory. *Ageing & Society, 27,* 599–614. http://dx.doi.org/10.1017/S0144686X07006009

Simpson, J. R. (2014). DSM–5 and neurocognitive disorders. *The Journal of the American Academy of Psychiatry and the Law, 42,* 159–164.

Sirey, J. A., Halkett, A., Chambers, S., Salamone, A., Bruce, M. L., Raue, P. J., & Berman, J. (2015). PROTECT: A pilot program to integrate mental health treatment into elder abuse services for older women. *Journal of Elder Abuse & Neglect, 27,* 438–453. http://dx.doi.org/10.1080/08946566.2015.1088422

Smits, A., Van Gaalen, R. I., & Mulder, C. H. (2010). Parent–child coresidence: Who moves in with whom and for whose needs? *Journal of Marriage and Family, 72,* 1022–1033. http://dx.doi.org/10.1111/j.1741-3737.2010.00746.x

Snyder, J. (2012). A partnership between adult protective services and Wachovia leads to a replicable nationwide model to spot and prevent financial abuse. *Generations: Journal of the American Society on Aging, 36*(2), 98–100.

Solomon, J., & Reingold, D. A. (2012). Creating an elder abuse shelter: A best-practice model for nonprofit nursing homes. *Generations: Journal of the American Society on Aging, 36*(3), 64–65.

Sommerfeld, D. H., Henderson, L. B., Snider, M. A., & Aarons, G. A. (2014). Multi-dimensional measurement within adult protective services: Design and initial testing of the tool for risk, interventions, and outcomes. *Journal of Elder Abuse & Neglect, 26,* 495–522. http://dx.doi.org/10.1080/08946566.2014.917598

Sorenson, S. B., & Shen, H. (2005). Restraining orders in California: A look at state-wide data. *Violence Against Women, 11,* 912–933. http://dx.doi.org/10.1177/1077801205276944

Steinmetz, S. K. (1978). Battered parents. *Society, 15*(5), 54–55. http://dx.doi.org/10.1007/BF02701616

Swanson, J., & Brownell, P. (2013). United States of America. In A. Phelan (Ed.), *International perspectives on elder abuse* (pp. 206–221). New York, NY: Routledge.

Szanton, S. L., Allen, J. K., Thorpe, R. J., Jr., Seeman, T., Bandeen-Roche, K., & Fried, L. P. (2008). Effect of financial strain on mortality in community-dwelling older women. *The Journals of Gerontology: Series B. Psychological Sciences and Social Sciences, 63*(6), S369–S374. http://dx.doi.org/10.1093/geronb/63.6.S369

Tarasoff v. Regents of the University of California, 551 P.2d 334 (Cal. 1976).

Taylor, B. J., Killick, C., O'Brien, M., Begley, E., & Carter-Anand, J. (2014). Older people's conceptualization of elder abuse and neglect. *Journal of Elder Abuse & Neglect, 26,* 223–243. http://dx.doi.org/10.1080/08946566.2013.795881

Teaster, P., Dugar, T., Mendiondo, M., Abner, E., Cecil, K., & Otto, J. (2006). *The 2004 survey of state adult protective services: Abuse of adults 60 years of age and older.* Washington, DC: National Center on Elder Abuse.

Teaster, P. B., Ramsey-Klawsnik, H., Abner, E. L., & Kim, S. (2015). The sexual victimization of older women living in nursing homes. *Journal of Elder Abuse & Neglect, 27,* 392–409. http://dx.doi.org/10.1080/08946566.2015.1082453

Teaster, P. B., Wangmo, T., & Anetzberger, G. J. (2010). A glass half full: The dubious history of elder abuse policy. *Journal of Elder Abuse & Neglect, 22,* 6–15. http://dx.doi.org/10.1080/08946560903436130

Terracina, K. A., Aamodt, W. W., & Schillerstrom, J. E. (2015). Executive function impairment and recidivism in adult protective services clients referred for a decision making capacity assessment. *Journal of Elder Abuse & Neglect*, *27*, 91–99. http://dx.doi.org/10.1080/08946566.2014.976894

Thomson, M. J., Lietzau, L. K., Doty, M. M., Cieslik, L., Williams, R., & Meurer, L. N. (2011). An analysis of elder abuse rates in Milwaukee County. *WMJ: Official Publication of the State Medical Society of Wisconsin*, *110*(6), 271–276.

Tronetti, P. (2014). Evaluating abuse in the patient with dementia. *Clinics in Geriatric Medicine*, *30*, 825–838. http://dx.doi.org/10.1016/j.cger.2014.08.010

Truman, J., & Langton, L. (2014). *Criminal victimization, 2013* (No. 247648). Washington, DC: Bureau of Justice Statistics, Office of Justice Programs, U.S. Department of Justice.

Tymula, A., Rosenberg Belmaker, L. A., Ruderman, L., Glimcher, P. W., & Levy, I. (2013). Like cognitive function, decision making across the life span shows profound age-related changes. *Proceedings of the National Academy of Sciences of the United States of America*, *110*, 17143–17148. http://dx.doi.org/10.1073/pnas.1309909110

U.S. Census Bureau. (2012). *The next four decades: The older population in the United States: 2010 to 2050* (pp. 25–1138). Washington, DC: Author.

U.S. Government Accountability Office. (2010). *Guardianships: Cases of financial exploitation, neglect, and abuse of seniors* (GAO-10-1046). Washington, DC: Author.

U.S. Government Accountability Office. (2011, March). *Elder justice: Stronger federal leadership could enhance national response to elder abuse* (GAO-11-208). Washington, DC: Author.

U.S. Senate Special Committee on Aging. (2011). *Justice for all: Ending elder abuse, neglect and financial exploitation*. Washington, DC: U.S. Government Printing Office.

U.S. Senate Special Committee on Aging. (2015). *Broken trust: Combating financial exploitation of vulnerable seniors*. Washington, DC: U.S. Government Printing Office.

Van Duizend, R. (2008). *The implications of an aging population for the state courts*. Future Trends in State Courts. Williamsburg, VA: National Center for State Courts.

Van Wielingen, L. E., Tuokko, H. A., Cramer, K., Mateer, C. A., & Hultsch, D. F. (2004). Awareness of financial skills in dementia. *Aging & Mental Health*, *8*, 374–380. http://dx.doi.org/10.1080/13607860410001709728

Verkerk, M. (1999). A care perspective on coercion and autonomy. *Bioethics*, *13*, 358–368. http://dx.doi.org/10.1111/1467-8519.00163

Vermont Statutes Annotated, Reports of Abuse, Neglect, and Exploitation of Vulnerable Adults, 33 V.S.A. § 6902(14) (2016).

Victor, C. (2005). The epidemiology of ageing. In M. L. Johnson (Ed.), *The Cambridge handbook of age and ageing* (pp. 95–105). http://dx.doi.org/10.1017/CBO9780511610714.009

Virginia Code Annotated, Adult Protective Services, Va. Code Ann. § 63.2-1606(A) (2017a).

Virginia Code Annotated, Adult Protective Services, Va. Code Ann. § 63.2-1606(E) (2017b).

Virginia Code Annotated, Adult Protective Services, Va. Code Ann. § 63.2-1606(H) (2017c).

Von Heydrich, L., Schiamberg, L. B., & Chee, G. (2012). Social-relational risk factors for predicting elder physical abuse: An ecological bi-focal model. *The International Journal of Aging & Human Development, 75*, 71–94. http://dx.doi.org/10.2190/AG.75.1.f

Wang, J. J. (2006). Psychological abuse and its characteristic correlates among elderly Taiwanese. *Archives of Gerontology and Geriatrics, 42*, 307–318. http://dx.doi.org/10.1016/j.archger.2005.08.006

Wenger, G. C. (2002). Interviewing older people. In J. F. Gubrium & J. A. Holstein (Eds.), *Handbook of interview research: Context and method* (pp. 259–278). Thousand Oaks, CA: Sage.

Wiglesworth, A., Kemp, B., & Mosqueda, L. (2008). Combating elder and dependent adult mistreatment: The role of the clinical psychologist. *Journal of Elder Abuse & Neglect, 20*, 207–230. http://dx.doi.org/10.1080/08946560801973051

Wiglesworth, A., Mosqueda, L., Mulnard, R., Liao, S., Gibbs, L., & Fitzgerald, W. (2010). Screening for abuse and neglect of people with dementia. *Journal of the American Geriatrics Society, 58*, 493–500. http://dx.doi.org/10.1111/j.1532-5415.2010.02737.x

Wilber, K. H., & McNeilly, D. P. (2001). Elder abuse and victimization. In J. E. Birren & K. W. Schaie (Eds.), *Handbook of the psychology of aging* (5th ed., pp. 569–591). San Diego, CA: Academic Press.

Wilber, K. H., & Reynolds, S. L. (1997). Introducing a framework for defining financial abuse of the elderly. *Journal of Elder Abuse & Neglect, 8*, 61–80. http://dx.doi.org/10.1300/J084v08n02_06

Winick, B. J. (1995). The side effects of incompetency labeling and the implications for mental health law. *Psychology, Public Policy, and Law, 1*(1), 6–42. http://dx.doi.org/10.1037/1076-8971.1.1.6

Wolf, R. S. (2001). Understanding elder abuse and neglect. In A. J. Walker, M. Manoogian-O'Dell, L. A. McGraw, & D. L. White (Eds.), *Families in later life: Connections and transitions* (pp. 258–261). Thousand Oaks, CA: Pine Forge Press.

Wood, E. F. (2006, August). *State-level adult guardianship data: An exploratory survey.* Washington, DC: National Center on Elder Abuse.

Wood, S., & Lichtenberg, P. A. (2017). Financial capacity and financial exploitation of older adults: Research findings, policy recommendations and clinical implications. *Clinical Gerontologist, 40*(1), 3–13. http://dx.doi.org/10.1080/07317115.2016.1203382

World Health Organization. (2015). #YearsAhead and valued—Participate in our Instagram campaign. Retrieved from http://www.who.int/ageing/features/yearsahead-campaign/en/

Wright, J. L. (2010). Guardianship for your own good: Improving the well-being of respondents and wards in the USA. *International Journal of Law and Psychiatry, 33*, 350–368. http://dx.doi.org/10.1016/j.ijlp.2010.09.007

Wu, L., Chen, H., Hu, Y., Xiang, H., Yu, X., Zhang, T., . . . Wang, Y. (2012). Prevalence and associated factors of elder mistreatment in a rural community in People's Republic of China: A cross-sectional study. *PLoS ONE, 7*(3), e33857. http://dx.doi.org/10.1371/journal.pone.0033857

Yaffe, M. J., Wolfson, C., Lithwick, M., & Weiss, D. (2008). Development and validation of a tool to improve physician identification of elder abuse: The Elder Abuse Suspicion Index (EASI). *Journal of Elder Abuse & Neglect, 20*, 276–300. http://dx.doi.org/10.1080/08946560801973168

Yan, E. (2014). Abuse of older persons with dementia by family caregivers: Results of a 6-month prospective study in Hong Kong. *International Journal of Geriatric Psychiatry, 29*, 1018–1027. http://dx.doi.org/10.1002/gps.4092

Yan, E., Chan, K. L., & Tiwari, A. (2015). A systematic review of prevalence and risk factors for elder abuse in Asia. *Trauma, Violence, & Abuse, 16*, 199–219. http://dx.doi.org/10.1177/1524838014555033

Yan, E., & Kwok, T. (2011). Abuse of older Chinese with dementia by family caregivers: An inquiry into the role of caregiver burden. *International Journal of Geriatric Psychiatry, 26*, 527–535. http://dx.doi.org/10.1002/gps.2561

Yllo, K., & Bogard, M. (Eds.). (1998). *Feminist perspectives on wife abuse.* Newbury Park, CA: Sage.

Zeranski, L., & Halgin, R. P. (2011). Ethical issues in elder abuse reporting: A professional psychologist's guide. *Professional Psychology: Research and Practice, 42*, 294–300. http://dx.doi.org/10.1037/a0023625

Ziminski, C. E., Wiglesworth, A., Austin, R., Phillips, L. R., & Mosqueda, L. (2013). Injury patterns and causal mechanisms of bruising in physical elder abuse. *Journal of Forensic Nursing, 9*(2), 84–91. http://dx.doi.org/10.1097/JFN.0b013e31827d51d0

Ziminski Pickering, C. E., & Phillips, L. R. (2014). Development of a causal model for elder mistreatment. *Public Health Nursing, 31*, 363–372. http://dx.doi.org/10.1111/phn.12108

Index

About the Author

Shelly L. Jackson, PhD, is a visiting assistant professor in the Institute of Law, Psychiatry and Public Policy, Department of Psychiatry and Neurobehavioral Sciences, at the University of Virginia. As a developmental psychologist, Dr. Jackson began her career in child maltreatment. In 2006, she and her colleague, Thomas L. Hafemeister, received a grant from the National Institute of Justice to study whether and how different forms of elder abuse are distinct—a grant that launched her interest in elder abuse. Dr. Jackson has since published numerous articles on elder abuse and frequently presents at professional conferences. Her teaching and research have focused on vulnerable victims (i.e., children, older adults, and incarcerated persons). Dr. Jackson received her doctoral training in developmental psychology from the University of Vermont and completed a postdoctoral fellowship in psychology and law at the University of Nebraska–Lincoln. In 1998, she was a Society for Research in Child Development Executive Branch Policy Fellow.